Sunshine Coast
Recreation
& Visitor's
Guide

Sunshine & Salt Air

Sunshine Coast
Recreation & Visitor's Guide

Sunshine & Salt Air

Edited by Peter A. Robson,
written by Karen Southern (upper Sunshine Coast) and
Bryan Carson (lower Sunshine Coast),
with Dorothy and Bodhi Drope, David Lee, Peter A. Robson,
Keith Thirkell and Howard White.

HARBOUR PUBLISHING

Harbour Publishing
P.O. Box 219
Madeira Park, BC Canada V0N 2H0
www.harbourpublishing.com

Cover, page design and composition by Roger Handling, Terra Firma Digital Arts.
Front and back cover photos by Keith Thirkell.
Printed and bound in Canada

Canadian Cataloguing in Publication Data

Carson, Bryan, 1941-
  Sunshine & salt air

  ISBN 1-55017-143-7

  1. Outdoor recreation—British Columbia—Sunshine Coast—Guidebooks. 2.
Outdoor Recreation—British Columbia—Powell River (Regional
district)—Guidebooks. 3. Sunshine Coast (B.C.)—Guidebooks. 4. Powell
River (B.C.: Regional district)—Guidebooks. I. Southern, Karen. II. Title.
GV191.46.B7C37 1997   917.11'31   C96-910055-8

Photo Contributors:
Elizabeth Abbott, 54, 58, 116, 146, 151; **William Abbott**, 65, 132, 133, 148, 158;
Carole Bowes, 131; **Leslie Burns**, 167, 169; **Fran Burnside**, 8; **Bryan Carson**, 70;
City of Vancouver Archives, 14 (BO.P.315,N-163), 52 (CVA 374-173);
Bob Coval/Emerald Sea Diving Adventures, 129; **Elphinstone Pioneer Museum**, 28,
104; **Heather Harbord**, 135; **Charlaine Lacroix**, 17; **Sean Percy**, 177;
Sean Percy/Powell River News, 125; **Tim Poole**, 137; **Powell River Historical
Museum Association**, 139 (3662), 142 (345), 143 (Rod LeMay 10430E), 165, 168;
Donnie Reid/Ocean Photography, 68, 98; **Rockwood Centre**, 53;
Peter A. Robson, 27, 29, 30, 31, 42, 48, 49, 51, 55, 57, 72, 79, 90, 95, 101, 103, 109;
Karen Southern, 112, 118, 138, 140, 144, 145, 146, 147, 153, 154, 164;
Keith Thirkell, 3, 9, 25, 11, 12, 15, 18, 20, 22, 24, 33, 38, 39, 43, 59, 60, 63, 73, 74, 87, 89,
105, 108, 114, 115, 166, 170, 175, 178, 180, 181, 183, 184, 185, 187, 188, 189, 190, 191;
Jim Willoughby, 67, 113.

PART 1
WELCOME TO THE SUNSHINE COAST • 9

PART 2
THE LOWER SUNSHINE COAST • 25

Port Mellon, Langdale and Gibsons • 25

Roberts Creek • 42

Sechelt • 49

Halfmoon Bay • 72

1

WELCOME TO THE SUNSHINE COAST

From downtown Vancouver, all it takes to get to the Sunshine Coast is a half-hour drive and a 40-minute sea voyage through some of the world's most impressive scenery. As the ferry churns the clear green waters of Howe Sound into white foam, you leave behind a city which attracts millions of tourists every year with its natural beauty and cultural richness. But those who long for the less hectic pace of a wilderness paradise can't do better than pay a visit to the Sunshine Coast.

As the crow flies, from Langdale to Lund, the Sunshine Coast is about 160 km (100 mi) long. But seen from a pleasure boat, canoe or kayak, or measured from a hiking trail travelled by boot or mountain bike, it seems like thousands of miles of intimate coves and secluded beaches.

The recreational opportunities are countless. Whether your taste runs to strenuous outdoor recreation or lounging on the patio, fine dining or hot dogs over an open fire, scuba diving, power boating or paddling, saltwater

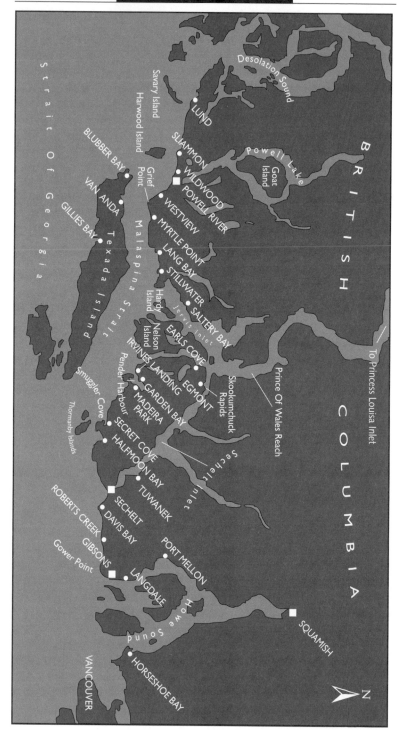

Desolation Sound

Strait of Georgia

Savary Island

Harwood Island

LUND

BLUBBER BAY

SLIAMMON

Grief Point

WILDWOOD

POWELL RIVER

Powell Lake

Goat Island

BRITISH COLUMBIA

VAN ANDA

WESTVIEW

GILLIES BAY

Malaspina Strait

MYRTLE POINT

LANG BAY

Texada Island

STILLWATER

Hardy Island

SALTERY BAY

Jervis Inlet

Nelson Island

EARLS COVE

Smuggler Cove

IRVINES LANDING

EGMONT

Skookumchuck Rapids

Prince Of Wales Reach

Thormanby Islands

Pender Harbour

GARDEN BAY

MADEIRA PARK

SECRET COVE

HALFMOON BAY

Sechelt Inlet

To Princess Louisa Inlet

ROBERTS CREEK

TUWANEK

SECHELT

DAVIS BAY

GIBSONS

PORT MELLON

Gower Point

LANGDALE

SQUAMISH

Howe Sound

VANCOUVER

HORSESHOE BAY

N

or freshwater fishing, cross country skiing, taking photographs or home videos of wildlife, relaxing in a fine hotel or camping under the stars, you can find it on the Sunshine Coast.

The elements that make the Coast so attractive to visitors can also be intimidating: the meandering roads confuse even the best-developed sense of direction; some trails run relentlessly uphill or downhill; beach accesses can be hard to find. There's so much water ... but where do we go paddling, hiking, mountain-biking? Where's the best swimming and scuba diving? Where can we camp?

Sunshine and Salt Air has the answers.

The first part of the book follows the highway from Langdale to Earls Cove (the lower Sunshine Coast) and across Jervis Inlet; the second part follows the highway from Saltery Bay to Powell River and Lund (the upper Sunshine Coast).

One of the coast's hundreds of bald eagles surveys its domain.

Earlier editions of *Sunshine and Salt Air* concentrated mainly on outdoor recreation. This new, expanded edition includes even more general visitor information, and many new features such as community histories, accommodation, dining and entertainment information, motoring tips, fascinating notes on coastal curiosities and a new section on off-road travel, as well as a full range of basic outdoor recreation information.

The Sunshine Coast boasts a spectacular range of wildlife and scenery. Bald eagles and other large raptors like turkey vultures and osprey are seen nearly every day. Blacktail deer are so plentiful they can be a traffic hazard. Roosevelt elk once came close to taking over the Pender Harbour golf course. The annual Christmas bird count routinely discovers more than 100 species and 17,000 or more individual birds. But you will not need to hunt for the wonders described here—they will come to you.

If you are camping here in the summer, prepare to be verbally harassed by Steller's jays, scolded by Douglas squirrels, and if you don't keep an eye out, raided in the friendliest sort of way by crows, ravens and raccoons. Those long gooey-looking things gliding around your campsite are some of the world's largest slugs.

While boating you will see and be observed by seals and sea lions and, if you are lucky, killer whales (orcas) and dolphins.

Dedicated birders who know where, when and how to look may add Virginia rails to their life lists.

If you venture off the beaten track you may see (and avoid) black bears, grizzlies and mountain goats. And there are cougars here. One of the authors has several times surprised bobcats in his yard. For the serious naturalist, there are numerous guides to trees, plants and wildlife that will add to your enjoyment of the outdoor experience. For an excellent overview of the people and history of the Sunshine Coast we suggest *The Sunshine Coast*, a full-colour coffee-table book by award-winning local author Howard White (Harbour Publishing, 1996).

This is the Sunshine Coast. We who are privileged to live here are privileged to welcome you. Enjoy! And please leave everything just as beautiful as you found it.

A Little Urban Geography

Urban geographers call the Sunshine Coast a "ribbon community." Stretched out along the Sunshine Coast Highway (101) are dozens of municipalities and communities, each with its own character and proud of it.

There are four local governments on the lower part of the Sunshine Coast: The Town of Gibsons (also referred to as Gibsons Landing, or simply Gibsons), The Sechelt Indian Government District, more often referred to as the Sechelt Indian Band (SIB), The District of Sechelt (or just Sechelt), and the Sunshine Coast Regional District, (SCRD).

Remote Phantom Lake, inland from the head of Salmon Inlet,
is one of the coast's scenic jewels.

North of Jervis Inlet in the Saltery Bay/Powell River area you will find another municipality, another regional district, the Sliammon Indian Village and other communities.

To further complicate matters there are communities within communities: Pender Harbour, for example, consists of Irvines Landing, Garden Bay, Kleindale and Madeira Park. Sechelt contains the communities of Davis Bay, Wilson Creek, Selma Park, Sandy Hook and Tuwanek.

The southern portion of the Powell River Regional District is made up of Saltery Bay, Stillwater, Lang Bay, Black Point, Myrtle Point and Pebble Beach. The District of Powell River was formed with the amalgamation of two villages: Westview and Cranberry with the company townsite and the rural area of Wildwood. Here also are Grief Point and Edgehill, communities within communities.

Texada Island, with its communities of Van Anda, Blubber Bay and Gillies Bay, lies across Malaspina Strait from much of the Sunshine Coast. With Southview, Savary Island, Okeover and Lund at the north end, that's pretty well the entire Sunshine Coast.

Why Is It Called the Sunshine Coast?

Some say the name was used first as a tourist gimmick by the Union Steamships and later the Blackball Ferries to attract customers. This may be true, but the name did not originate there. It was claimed much earlier by Harry Roberts of Roberts Creek when he painted "Sunshine Belt" on the side of the first freight shed on the first wharf in Roberts Creek in the 1920s or earlier. Roberts said it was his grandmother's wish to name the place the Sunshine Belt. A real estate agent in Gibsons added the "Coast" sometime after 1930.

The Daddy Boats:
The Era Before the Ferries

"Carrying passengers and groceries into virtually every nook and cranny on the BC coast, ships of the Union Steamships' fleet provide a tangible link from southern civilization to the far northern suburbs," wrote Jack Hetherington in his "Ship Shop" column in the *North Vancouver Times*.

The development of the Sunshine Coast is intimately tied to the Union Steamship Company, one of the original links between the Peninsula and Vancouver. In fact, some claim that Harold Brown, general manager and later president of the company, originated the term "Sunshine Coast." In fact, he simply popularized it, through advertisements for the company's Vancouver to Savary Island sailings.

As early as 1890, the 180-foot *Cutch* was running excursions to Gibsons Landing and Pender Harbour. In 1920, the *Capilano II* made her trial trip to the company's resort in Selma Park just south of Sechelt, carrying 300 passengers. The *"Cap"* began tri-weekly trips to Selma Park via Gibsons and

The Daddy Boat's coming! The Union Steamship Company was the form of transport for many years.

Roberts Creek, and on weekends took picnickers to Halfmoon Bay and Buccaneer Bay on the Thormanby Islands.

The Selma Park resort was situated approximately where the boat launch is in present-day Selma Park, and included 20 cottages, several campsites, a picnic area, a tearoom and a dance pavilion. It was such a success that in 1926, the company took over the bankrupt Herbert Whittaker's hotel, store, wharf and resort fronting Trail Bay in Sechelt.

By 1925, the *Lady Cecilia* and her sister ship the *Lady Cynthia* had begun regular service to Pender Harbour and beyond to Powell River and Lund. Each ship could carry 800 passengers and took only six hours to make the passage. The area was also served by the SS *Cowichan* and SS *Chelohsin*.

The Friday afternoon sailings were dubbed the "Daddy boats" because so many of their passengers were fathers who worked in Vancouver and came to the Coast on weekends to be with their vacationing families.

The war years were difficult for the company and the Sechelt resort was sold in 1944. Improved roads and ferry service from Horseshoe Bay to Langdale (starting in 1951) took their toll, and steamship service was reduced and later eliminated.

By 1959 the steamship line had lost its federal subsidy. The facilities were sold, and residents of coastal settlements no longer saw the familiar red and black funnels that had linked the area to the mainland for so many years.

A Climate Where Forests and Gardens Abound

The Sunshine Coast is a haven for gardeners and wildflower enthusiasts. Gardeners revel in one of the warmest growing zones in Canada (Zone 8A). For botanists, the area's characteristics range from those of the Coast Forest biotic zone to those of the Gulf Islands biotic zone, the main difference between them being the amount of rainfall—254 cm (100″) in the Coast Forest zone in contrast with about 76 cm (30″) in the Gulf Island zone. The Forest Service, not to be outdone, defines much of the Sunshine Coast as part of the Maritime Coastal Western Hemlock biogeoclimatic zone.

Anyone who lives here during the blessedly short winter knows it is a rain forest.

In his well-known field guide *Trees, Shrubs and Flowers to Know in British Columbia*, C.P. Lyons points out that the Gulf Islands biotic zone is home to the most varied flora in the province. He lists 228 trees, 48 shrubs and 87 flowers commonly found in the area.

The Caren Range, the mountain spine of the Sechelt Peninsula, is said to support the oldest forest in Canada, one which has survived some 10,000 years without major disturbance. One yellow cedar (cypress) stump was recently determined to be over 1,800 years old.

The mainstay of the forests of the Sunshine Coast are Douglas fir and red cedar. Douglas fir prefers drier areas and can grow as high as 120 m (400 ft) and well over 3 m (10 ft) in diameter. Its wood produces some of the strongest and largest pieces of lumber in the world. Red cedar grows to even broader

Yes, the trees really are that big. Seen here is an old-growth Douglas fir.

diameters of 4 m (13 ft) or more and prefers slightly wetter conditions than fir. As lumber, cedar is known for its great rot-resistant qualities and its suitability for roofing shakes and shingles. Low-quality logs of both species are used in pulp operations.

The most common deciduous species on the Sunshine Coast are alder and broadleaf maple. Alder is extremely prolific and is usually the first tree species to sprout in a fresh clearing. It seldom lives longer than 100 years. Broadleaf maple is not so prolific, tends to prefer wetter areas, and can live for several hundred years. Both species serve a valuable role in soil health by fixing nitrogen into the soil through their roots and decaying leaves.

Neither species has much commercial value as lumber, but both are used in the manufacture of furniture and firewood.

Today when you drive up the Sunshine Coast Highway you can admire mile after mile of towering trees on both sides of the road and off into the distance. It is hard to believe that virtually every accessible hectare of the Sunshine Coast was logged during the past 100 years, and that those magnificent, healthy trees we see today are the result of nature's incredible regenerative ability.

Which North is That?

The Sunshine Coast generally runs southeast–northwest. Except where it's interrupted by Jervis Inlet—where you have to take another ferry— the Sunshine Coast Highway (101) more or less parallels the coastline, which is to say it meanders. To keep things simple, in this book we call any direction up the coast, towards Lund, "north," and any direction down the coast, towards Gibsons, "south." Like many things on the coast, this is wildly inaccurate, but as you'll find out when you're here, it works.

Please Tread Lightly

The wilderness is vast, but diminishing. We used to take for granted that it was ours and that it was endless. Now we realize we are sharing it not only with each other, but with creatures who have as much right to it as human beings.

Garbage: It is *not* okay to leave your garbage behind. Please tread lightly and leave no trace of your passing. Many people carry a spare plastic bag in case they need to clean up after someone else. Take your cans and bottles with you when you leave, and above all, if you like to travel with a six-pack, do not discard the plastic doodad that holds the cans together. These can be lethal to wildlife. You may remember that gruesome picture on the local news of a seal caught in a six-pack holder, its muzzle worn raw and bleeding, doomed to die of starvation, infection or loss of blood.

Campfires: Campfires can be a dangerous indulgence in forests that are powder dry for much of the summer. Fires must be very small, built on a mineral base, always attended and *dead, dead, dead* before you leave them. During dry periods, there is often a ban on campfires. Make sure you know which fire protection district you are in and which regulations are in effect. To report a forest fire, call 1-800-663-5555. People who cause forest fires can be held responsible for the cost of fighting them.

Wildlife: Respect it, all of it, and leave it as you find it. Some creatures may sneak past you to help themselves to your provisions, but do not deliberately feed animals or birds. Don't pick the flowers. The flower may be the plant's survival tool. Berries are a different matter—once you are sure which ones are edible, help yourself.

*A small herd of elk, introduced to the Sunshine Coast
20 years ago, is expanding quickly.*

Licences and limits: Many of the activities described in this book will lead you into a land of apparently unlimited bounty—beaches and rocks covered with oysters and mussels; congregations of littleneck and butter clams under a few inches of sand; beds of swimming scallops; lakes teeming with trout. The resource, however, is no longer unlimited, nor is your right to it. There are licence, size and bag restrictions that apply to all of these. Hunting and fishing regulations are available free of charge at sporting goods stores and government offices. You need one licence to fish in tidal water (the ocean) and a second for non-tidal water (streams and lakes).

Private property: Respect it. When we know a trail or access passes through privately owned land, we have noted it. If the directions say obtain permission, please do it. This also applies to the place where you park your car. Please do not harass or feed livestock, and leave all gates the way you found them.

Four Words on Safety: It's Up to You

Know enough about your chosen activity to do it safely. Take the best advice available from someone who knows. If you are planning an excursion in the woods or on the water, tell someone where you are going and how long you plan to be out, and contact them as soon as you return. There are no monsters here that are out to get you, but this is wild country.

Dress for it: This is a rain forest—you will get wet. Usually this is not a problem in the summer, but in colder weather, it can lead to hypothermia for hikers, bikers and paddlers who are not prepared. Pack a poncho and feel smug if it rains.

If you get lost: Don't panic. Get warm, collect your thoughts, review your outdoor survival training and select the most appropriate strategy. The part of the Sunshine Coast this book covers is sufficiently narrow any healthy adult can walk across it in a day as long as they walk in a straight line. If you are on the water, there are few places other boats aren't going past occasionally. Position yourself where your signal can be seen and wait. Presumably, you took our advice and told someone where you were going.

Red Tide: Paralytic Shellfish Poisoning micro-organisms are fairly common on the coast in the summer months, rendering shellfish unfit for human consumption and lethal in certain cases. Warnings are usually posted when necessary. Check with locals. You can also check the local papers or, if you can find anyone in, the Department of Fisheries and Oceans. Their number on the lower Sunshine Coast is 883-2313, upper Sunshine Coast is 485-7963.

Water pollution: There is some coliform and industrial pollution on some parts of the coast. Some of the tastiest-looking oysters grow in the most polluted waters. Fresh-looking mountain streams are not always potable and can cause illness. Carry water with you or use purifying tablets.

Don't argue with one of these. It has the right of way.

Logging roads: Many of the hikes and bike trails we describe follow active logging roads. There are usually signs indicating when the road is available for public use. If you've ever seen a loaded logging truck roaring down a mountain, you will agree that it makes good sense to keep out of its way. Note that signs identifying logging roads are usually located a short way up the logging road, not on the highway.

Bears: The Sunshine Coast has a large population of black bears. They may look cute from a distance, but they are *not* your friends. Given the opportunity, they will avoid you, but many have learned that campers and hikers carry food, which they can smell from a great distance if it is not properly stored.

One hint: don't be too quiet while hiking. Some hikers attach small bells to their gear. This gives a bear enough warning of your presence to allow it a dignified exit.

While grizzly (sometimes called brown) bears are a rarity on the lower Sunshine Coast, they have been seen around Jervis and Narrows inlets and on the upper Sunshine Coast.

Poisonous snakes: Relax, there are none.

Wood ticks: The Pacific wood tick is the most common tick on the Sunshine Coast. Diseases caused by ticks are rare here and throughout BC. Still, ticks can be among the most revolting pests you will encounter, since you often don't notice them until they have burrowed partway into your skin.

Ticks live in tall grass and wooded areas and can crawl onto your clothing and skin when you brush up against foliage. Stay on cleared paths whenever possible. Tuck your clothing in, use insect repellent and wear light-coloured clothing.

Ticks start out about the size of a sesame seed. When they find a host, they pierce the skin and extract blood, inflating their bodies. They appear as a grayish-blue blob on the surface of the skin and drop off when they've had their fill. An engorged tick is about the size of an unshelled sunflower seed.

A sore spot on your body will usually give away a tick's location. Check yourself and your companions when you have been in tall grass or the forest. Check your pets too. Experienced tick-pullers simply grasp the tick close to its head with their thumb and forefingers and twist and pull at the same time. For the squeamish, use tweezers and gently grasp the tick as close to the head as you can and pull the tick straight out. Treat the bite with alcohol. Check with your doctor for further advice, especially if any portion of the tick remains in your body.

In cold weather: Wear several layers of light clothing so you can adjust according to the ambient temperature and your level of exertion. Some people like to feel a little chilly before they set out on a strenuous excursion, knowing they will soon warm up.

Eat: Hiking or paddling is a good excuse for lots of snacks and hot and cold drinks as well as a big dinner the night before and a hearty breakfast before setting out.

Don't overdo it: C'mon, you know your limits.

Why So Fast? The Metric System

If you are from the United States, you may wonder at our speed limits. Driving 80 on the Sunshine Coast Highway may seem like a real challenge.

But remember during the 1970s when President Gerald Ford signed the Metric Conversion Act? It decreed that North America would go metric, but didn't say when. Canada dutifully went on board and began the conversion process. There was such animosity toward the idea in the States that it was delayed—some say abandoned—leaving Canada stuck halfway through the change, a position that remains in effect to this day. While the metric system is the one kids are learning in school, anyone over age 40 still favours the old system.

All measurements in *Sunshine and Salt Air* are given first in metric, followed by the imperial equivalent in parentheses: 100 kph (60 mph).

Cycling on the Sunshine Coast

The Circle Route, so beloved of motorists, is also popular with recreational cyclists: from Vancouver via ferry to Langdale, up the peninsula to Earls Cove, another ferry to Saltery Bay, to Powell River, ferry to Comox on Vancouver Island, down the island to Nanaimo or Victoria and by ferry once again, back to Vancouver.

Geared up to take on a mountain trail.

Public and private campgrounds are spaced more or less conveniently along the way but these tend to fill up quickly during the summer months.

For mountain-bikers, we have presented a broad sampling of tried and true trails. An enthusiastic cadre of mountain bikers is constantly upgrading old and creating more trails. The main trails are shown in our maps here. These will lead you to more and more trails. A rule of thumb: the further UP they are, the more challenging. Please play nice as you'll be sharing these trails with horseback riders and hikers.

See the Appendix for information on obtaining bike parts and service.

Sport Fishing on the Sunshine Coast

Blame it on bad conservation practices, greed, environmental conditions, lack of international co-operation or the fish themselves. There just aren't as many as there used to be.

Say "fish" here and everyone understands you to mean salmon, much as "fish" on the east coast of Canada means cod.

Sports fishermen like to think the secret to the location of their favourite spots is known only to them, but once the fish start biting, the rumour of a "hot spot" quickly gets around. Find where the boats are clustered and join in. Marinas and tackle shops are usually pretty generous with fishing tips and local techniques.

Other species bite too. You may find lingcod and rockcod off some of the reefs.

Kids can have a great time fishing off government and public wharves. You'll find these in Gibsons, Roberts Creek, Davis Bay, Porpoise Bay, Halfmoon Bay, Secret Cove, Madeira Park, Irvines Landing, Egmont and Westview. Catches may include shiners, perch, rockfish and running shoes. The Davis Bay dock produces a surprising number of chinook salmon.

The lakes and streams also abound with rainbow and cutthroat trout, and many are stocked. Just about any lake will offer up the chance to catch one and many lakes are easily accessible by car. Again, check at tackle shops for info on the hot spots. Generally, the 4x4 access lakes have the better fishing.

Remember, licences are required—separate ones for saltwater and freshwater fishing. All stocks need to be conserved. Please pay close attention to size and bag limits.

Exploring the Sunshine Coast by Boat

Granted that the Sunshine Coast Highway has its own attractions, and leads to limitless places to hike, bike, camp and four-wheel, roads are still a fairly recent invention on the Sunshine Coast. In fact, it's not unreasonable to argue that the only way to know this or any coast is to get out on the water.

Every summer, the crowd coming off the ferry at Langdale seems to be matched by the number of visitors who arrive by kayak, cabin cruiser, sailboat or yacht. There are plenty of marinas where a trip ashore offers fuel, supplies, food, drink and entertainment, and of course the coast itself conceals innumerable bays, coves, inlets and islets where boaters can drop anchor and explore.

For more information about the many boat cruising opportunities, we suggest Bill Wolferstan's *Cruising Guide to British Columbia, Vol. 3: Sunshine Coast*, published by Whitecap Books.

Diving on the Sunshine Coast

Some of the best diving in BC, which is highly favoured by enthusiasts around the world, can be enjoyed in the waters surrounding the Sunshine Coast. *National Geographic* recognized the diving significance of Jervis Inlet and Saltery Bay in a 14-page feature article in April 1980. In 1988, the Cousteau Society spent three weeks in the area, filming the octopus.

Deep channels and large tidal changes ensure abundant nutrient-rich water is constantly being stirred up to feed the area's large variety of marine life, from plankton and sea anemones to herring and killer whales. The absence of any major rivers helps to ensure good underwater visibility, even during periods of high runoff. The best diving is during the winter when

*The Sunshine Coast has been called
the scuba diving capital of Canada.*

visibility-reducing plankton are minimal. Summer months see increased plankton growth in shallow waters. Below this layer, however, the deeper, cooler water is clear.

The Sunshine Coast is rich with opportunities for the diver. Sheer cliffs, shallow-water shipwrecks, underwater caves, and some of the world's largest octopus and wolf eels have all contributed greatly to the area's reputation as the scuba diving capital of Canada.

Highlights include Canada's first underwater statue, a dive site called Octopus City, opportunities to dive with sea lions and seals, shipwrecks that vary from a sailing ship to a destroyer, exciting cave diving and a myriad of multicoloured marine life. Look for wolf eels, nudibranchs, hydroids, anemones, tiny neon clown shrimp, and boot sponges that grow so large a diver can crawl inside. You may be lucky enough to see the rare .7 m (20") orange Puget Sound King Crab, a colourful creature with purple spots.

Many Sunshine Coast sites are boat access locations. Safe anchoring, exposed water and, in certain locations, currents are the biggest challenges. In addition to managing the logistics of the vessel, a boat master must be aware that fragile marine life can be damaged by anchors or ground tackle.

It is always best to have an anchored boat attended by a competent operator. When possible, keep the boat live. That way you can be more adventurous with your dive plan.

Don't forget to fly your dive flag when in the water. Responsible boaters will look for your signals and respond accordingly.

Shore diving opportunities on the Sunshine Coast are limited. Those most frequently visited are listed in the guide for each area. When exploring these or any other shore dive please respect the surrounding private property—parking, changing and toilet facilities will be limited, or zero. Respect laws restricting diving around public docks.

There are numerous opportunities to make advanced and technical dives on the Sunshine Coast. It is the responsibility of individual divers to plan their dives within the limits of their training and experience.

Wherever and whenever you dive, follow the old rule: take only pictures; leave only bubbles.

Dining on the Sunshine Coast

From stick-to-the-ribs hiker/biker fare to gourmet dining at its finest, Coast restaurants offer a full palette of gustatory experiences. Local seafood is featured at many of them.

Our listings by area include only the eateries that have been in business long enough to convince us they will still be around as you read this book. Most take major credit cards. The $ symbol indicates the relative price of a meal for two people.

Note that many pubs on the Sunshine Coast offer delicious pub grub.

Editor's Note:

The writers, editors and publishers of *Sunshine and Salt Air* have made every effort to ensure the reader's awareness of the accessibility, hazards and level of expertise involved in the activities described, but your own safety is ultimately up to you. We can take no responsibility for any loss or injury incurred by anyone using this book.

If you spot any inaccuracies, please let us know:

Sunshine and Salt Air
c/o Harbour Publishing Co. Ltd.
P.O. Box 219
Madeira Park, BC
V0N 2H0
e-mail: info@harbourpublishing.com

2

THE LOWER SUNSHINE COAST

PORT MELLON, LANGDALE & GIBSONS

The ferry trip from Vancouver to Langdale offers 45 minutes to relax, enjoy the scenery and plan at least the first few minutes of your visit to the Sunshine Coast. Upon docking, your first decision is whether to go left, right or straight ahead from the ferry terminal.

A right turn will take you to Port Mellon, site of the largest single employer on the lower Sunshine Coast, Howe Sound Pulp and Paper. Free tours of the mill are offered frequently during the summer months and provide an insight into one of the most modern and pollution-free pulp mills in

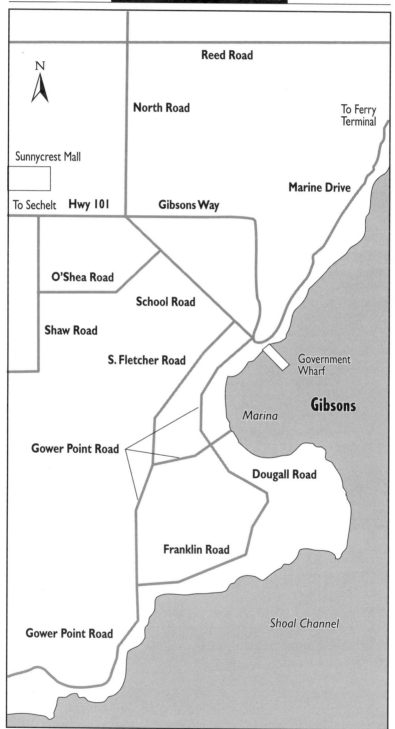

N

Reed Road

North Road

To Ferry
Terminal

Sunnycrest Mall

Marine Drive

To Sechelt   Hwy 101   Gibsons Way

O'Shea Road

School Road

Shaw Road

S. Fletcher Road

Government
Wharf

Gibsons

Marina

Gower Point Road

Dougall Road

Franklin Road

Gower Point Road

Shoal Channel

Your first decision on the Sunshine Coast must be a quick one. Turn left and you will immediately begin to experience the character of the Sunshine Coast.

BC. (Tours must be pre-booked. Phone 604-884-5223, local 575).

If you go straight ahead you'll be driving on the Gibsons Bypass—which merges with the Sunshine Coast Highway (Highway 101), to take you right to the heart of the coast—or left toward Gibsons.

We strongly recommend the left turn onto Marine Drive, which lets you begin to experience immediately the character of the Sunshine Coast.

The road, like most on the coast, is narrow, twisting and hilly. Family names on driveway signs are evidence of the relaxed summer-resort and cottage-country history of the area—a feeling that still pervades most of the coast.

Crowding down to the invisible beach below, among the impressive trunks of second-growth Douglas fir, gardens and lawns have been lovingly cultivated amid the salal and blackberry. Through the trees, you can see the sun glistening across the waters of Howe Sound, and fair-weather mooring buoys dot the shallows just off the beach.

Every yard seems to hold a canoe, car-topper or runabout. Nowadays these little boats are used purely for recreation—fishing or water-skiing or sightseeing—but it was not that long ago that a boat was a crucial transportation link to the world beyond the coast. In days when motors were expensive and unreliable, many pioneers rowed into Vancouver at regular intervals to pick up supplies, and as late as the 1950s many small communities did not have road access.

Even today, small boats remain the lifelines of the two large islands on either side of Gibsons—Gambier and Keats, which are served by a small pedestrian-only ferry.

Many of the small communities you will pass bear the names of early settlers. Hopkins Landing, for example, just past the ferry terminal, was named after George Henderson Hopkins, originally from County Down, Ireland, who acquired the land in 1906. He had intended to use it as a summer home, but he liked it so much he settled permanently and used his engineering expertise to design a well-planned hamlet. A little farther along is Granthams Landing, founded in 1909 by F.C. Grantham, a Vancouver businessman who launched a vigorous tradition of real estate speculation on the coast, although he never actually lived here.

Just past Granthams lies Gibsons, the southernmost incorporated municipality on the Sunshine Coast. It was named after George Gibson, who came here to homestead in 1886. Legend has it that the name was shortened from Gibsons Landing, as it was known for most of its existence, to Gibsons when the Post Office discovered that it was too long to fit on the standard cancellation stamp. A grassroots movement is underway to restore the original name; even if it founders, to many of us the town, especially the lower part, will always be Gibsons Landing.

GEORGE GIBSON

It was only by chance that in 1886 George Gibson and his two sons "discovered" the area which is now Gibsons. As the three were sailing from Nanaimo to Vancouver, a storm blew up and they sought shelter in a bay on Keats Island. The next day they sailed across to the headland, landing near what today is the government wharf. Gibson was so pleased with the site that he immediately pre-empted 160 acres on the waterfront. Two years later, much of the adjacent coast inland to the mountains had also been pre-empted. By the late 1990s, the population of Gibsons had grown to over 3,000.

As a result of car ferry service and new roads connecting the communities along the coast, Gibsons began to grow away from the waterfront. In time this created a townsite which is divided into two geographic areas, upper and lower Gibsons. Upper Gibsons has the shopping malls, subdivisions and condominiums, while lower Gibsons has the history and character: a variety of craft shops and galleries, an antique row, interesting restaurants and two pleasant walks, the sea walk and the Inglis trail.

The government wharf has been a centre of activity in Lower Gibsons for many years. All manner of craft come and go complete with crews of colourful characters. The tradition continues with an added attraction. In 2000 West Coast Log Homes completed work on wharf renovations including the new wharfinger's building—a magnificent structure made from local cedar logs. The logs themselves are massive yet the building is so artfully designed that the building seems extremely light and open. Definitely worth a look. While you are at the wharf you may want to take advantage of the fresh prawns, crabs, oysters and fish available from some of the boats.

The water is remarkably clear most of the time. Kids love fishing from the wharf, though catch-and-release is highly recommended. Beautiful

MOLLY'S REACH: FAMILIAR TO MILLIONS

Molly's Reach, at the head of the main wharf in Gibsons is familiar to millions of TV viewers from the long running *Beachcombers* series. Built before WWI the structure has seen service as a grocery store, furniture store, real estate and insurance office, hardware store and liquor store. Since the TV series began, in 1971 it has become the main landmark in lower Gibsons.

anemones growing on the pilings are visible through the clear water.

Just up from the floats, look for the huge "Welcome Back" sign on Molly's Reach, the central set of the long-running CBC TV series *The Beachcombers*. Visitors should allow at least several hours to explore Gibsons. If you are willing to put out a little energy for a breathtaking overview of the lower Sunshine Coast, try the Soames Hill hike. For an insight into Sunshine Coast history, take in the Elphinstone Pioneer Museum at 716 Winn Road. For a wide variety of antiques, clothing and local crafts try Molly's Lane just beside Molly's Reach.

A stroll along Marine Drive, in either direction from the wharf will take you to many fine eateries, shops and galleries.

The intersection of Highway 101 and School Road, in upper Gibsons, is the location of three heritage buildings: the old Schoolhouse, St. Bartholomew's Anglican Church, and Heritage Theatre. All three have recently been renovated. The theatre began as the Women's Institute Hall, had fallen into desuetude and took on its present form in the fall of 2000. Theatre buffs will want to look at it as an innovative performing space. Even better if you take in a play.

Somewhat out of the way, but worth stopping for is Gift of the Eagle Gallery at Highway 101 and Martin Road, (turn left off School Rd if you are coming up from lower Gibsons), and impressive collection of local arts and crafts.

Stonehurst: The Inglis House

The large white house with its imposing verandah, located at the bottom of School Road in lower Gibsons, has a significant place in the history not just of the Sunshine Coast, but of Canadian politics. The house, known as Stonehurst, was built by Dr. Fred Inglis when he arrived in Gibsons Landing in 1913, and for the next 30 years he operated his medical practice from its lower floor. Dr. Inglis was for many years the only physician for miles around, covering most of the Sunshine Coast by rowboat, horse and Model T Ford.

Because Dr. Inglis was a man of many passions, including social democratic politics, the big white house became a natural refuge for the new

Methodist minister, a man with pacifist leanings who arrived in Gibsons in 1917. When the minister lost his post for preaching against World War I, Dr. Inglis took in the man's wife and six children. The minister, James Shaver Woodsworth, went off to continue his work as an activist for social justice, eventually founding the Cooperative Commonwealth Federation (CCF), the most successful leftist political party in North American history.

Stonehurst—a heritage home and arguably the cradle of Canadian socialism.

One of the Woodsworth children who spent her early years in the Inglis house, Grace Woodsworth MacInnis, became British Columbia's first woman Member of Parliament. She returned to the area after retiring and died at Sechelt in 1991. Two of her brothers, Ralph and Bruce, also returned to spend their sunset years on the Sunshine Coast.

For two years in the 1970s, the Inglis house was the centre for an ambulance service. Later there were plans to turn it into a neighbourhood pub, but these plans did not materialize. Stonehurst is now being restored by private owners.

WALKS & BEACHES AROUND GIBSONS

The **Seawalk** follows the shoreline around Gibsons Harbour. The easiest access is from the stairs between the government dock and Molly's Reach. Turn left and stroll under the ramp to the dock; past Grandma's Pub; Cole's Marine Ways; Century House, originally built as three apartments by Dr. Fred Inglis and now a private home; the Rugby Club building, once Gibsons Landing's municipal hall; and emerge at Armour's Beach.

Alternatively, turn right from the stairs and stroll along the beach past the waterfront park and the plaque commemorating the arrival of George Gibson, founder of Gibsons Landing. The walk ends abruptly, but by turning right up the path onto Marine Drive and down again at the lane by the private residence with the steep red roof, you can continue along the shoreline, coming out near the Gibsons Yacht Club.

Dr. Fred Inglis is commemorated by the **Inglis Trail**, a short walk from upper to lower Gibsons. Its greatest virtue is that it is not steep like other roads in the area. To access the trail, or the Inglis House from the Sunshine Coast Highway, turn down Shaw Road at the traffic lights at Sunnycrest Mall. Follow Shaw to its end and look for the sign which commemorates Dr. Fred Inglis.

Public Beaches near Gibsons

Armours Beach: One of the few sandy beaches in the area, the swimming area is marked in the summer. The beach can be reached from the Seawalk or from Marine Drive, although parking is limited.

Georgia Beach: Take Prowse Bay Road to Georgia. Turn left onto Georgia and follow it to the bottom where there is parking for three or four cars. From the pebbled beach, the view looks over Shoal Channel to Keats Island. The park is operated by the Town of Gibsons and dogs are not allowed.

Pebbles Beach Park: A small, town-owned park at the end of Burns Road. Well-maintained steps lead to the pebble beach. Lots of logs for sitting and watching the activity in Shoal Channel.

Attlee's Beach Park: Follow the steps down to the water from the end of Cochrane Road. Parking is severely limited from this access.

Secret Beach: Follow Gower Point Road away from the town centre to Mahan Road. Watch for the Sunshine Coast Regional District park sign on the left hand side of the road. Stairs lead down to the beach.

Chaster Provincial Park: Follow Gower Point Road away from the town centre. On your left, as the road descends to water level at 6th Avenue, is Chaster Park, operated by the Sunshine Coast Regional District. There is

Logs, useful as backrests and impromptu picnic tables, have been thoughtfully provided at most coast beaches.

plenty of parking. On a clear night, you can see the bright lights on Vancouver Island. Along the beach is a cairn commemorating Captain George Vancouver's passage through the area.

HIKES AROUND GIBSONS

Soames Hill (The Knob)

This is the distinctive "knob" you see from the ferry as it approaches Langdale. Although the trail to the summit is well maintained, the hike is relentlessly "up." However, the view is so dramatic from the arbutus grove on top, you'll feel guilty if you whined about the climb. You'll see Georgia Strait, Gibsons, Howe Sound and even Point Grey on a clear day. You can watch the ferry come in, boats head in and out of Gibsons Harbour, and tugs heading up and down the coast. In short, you can see much that makes the Sunshine Coast so special.

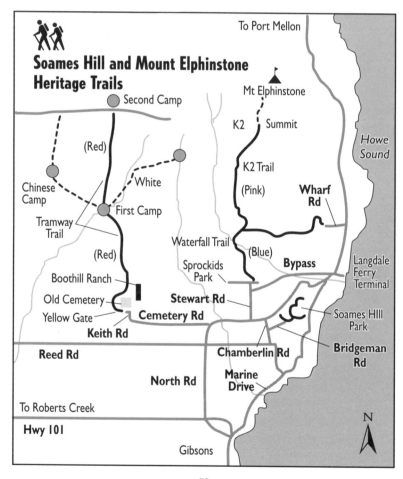

Soames Hill and Mount Elphinstone Heritage Trails

To Port Mellon

Mt Elphinstone

K2 | Summit

Howe Sound

Second Camp

(Red)

K2 Trail

(Pink)

Wharf Rd

Chinese Camp

White

First Camp

Tramway Trail

Waterfall Trail

(Blue)

Bypass

Langdale Ferry Terminal

(Red)

Sprockids Park

Boothill Ranch

Old Cemetery

Yellow Gate

Cemetery Rd

Stewart Rd

Soames Hill Park

Keith Rd

Reed Rd

Chamberlin Rd

Bridgeman Rd

North Rd

Marine Drive

To Roberts Creek

Hwy 101

N

Gibsons

Access: Take North Road in Gibsons toward Langdale to Chamberlin Road. Follow Chamberlin to Bridgeman Road and turn left. At Boyle Road you'll see the parking lot, well marked with Regional District signs.

Hiking Time: Allow about 40 minutes each way, and plenty of time to rest at the top.

Description: Intermediate. The trail begins at a parking lot and meanders along an old logging road for about 10 minutes. There is a "Y" in the road before you arrive at the steep part; keep to the right, the left fork dead ends. On your right, a trail leads straight up the hill. Pay attention, it's not well marked.

There are very few switchbacks along the trail; instead, steps have been built to get you up the steepest parts, some with handrails. As you make your way up you will notice old notched logs—the original steps. These were extremely slippery, and combined with the fact there were no handrails, they made the trail quite hazardous.

THE MOUNT ELPHINSTONE HERITAGE TRAILS

It is a little more than 100 years since George Gibson landed on what became known as the Sunshine Coast. Much of the history and economy since then have involved the harvest of the prime Douglas fir forests that once blanketed almost every square yard of this coast. Some of the earliest logging took place in the area around Gibsons and Mount Elphinstone. Walking through these areas logged up to a century ago, you cannot help notice how little evidence of that activity remains—a testament to the astonishing regenerative powers of the west coast rain forest.

Beginning in 1988, the Gibsons Landing Heritage Society (GLHS) under the direction of then President Fred W. Inglis began to map and mark the old logging trails. Existing ones were upgraded and new trails built to connect the old ones. The complex of trails is centred around the Stoltz Company's 1920s shinglebolt operation which was itself centred

STELLER'S JAY

The official bird of British Columbia, the Steller's jay is the comedian of the coniferous forest. The dark blue 33-cm (13-in) bird is the only crested jay found west of the Rocky Mountains. It is related to the blue jay, but it is larger and has no white on it, not even the white eyebrow of the inland race.

Very bold around people, the jay will perch in a nearby tree and demand its due with a loud *shack-shack-shack* sound. It's a common sight at campsites in the summer when the pickings are good, but in spring and fall it knows the whereabouts of every bird feeder in the area. Steller's jays are especially fond of unsalted peanuts and sunflower seeds.

around what came to be known as "First Camp." Shinglebolts (the blocks from which shingles are split) were transported to First Camp from other, smaller camps and then floated several miles down a raised flume to the sea in the vicinity of what is now the Langdale ferry terminal.

One important part of the trails upgrading project involved marking the trails with colour-coded aluminum markers. Most of the markers also include strips of reflective tape to make them easier to spot. If hikers get caught out after dark, the markers can be found by shining a flashlight at eye level.

But be careful, there is no guarantee that the markers will be in place—vandalism and the unstoppable march of the rain forest take their toll.

K2 (Summit Trail)

K2 is the abbreviation for Knob 2 (Knob 1 being Soames Hill). Plan for some R & R time when you get to the top so you can enjoy the panoramic view of Howe Sound, the Britannia Mountain Range, Vancouver and Vancouver Island.

Access: From the townsite of Langdale—on the highway north (right) from the BC Ferries terminal—head inland on Wharf Road, which soon degenerates into an oversized ditch. Park where you can. There are no diamond markers, but the trail is normally flagged with surveyor's tape.

Hiking Time: 2 hours plus, each way.

Description: Intermediate. After parking, begin walking up the roadbed. Arriving at the Hydro transmission wires, turn left, then head uphill when you come to a rough road. Your route winds through a "selectively" logged area, then temporarily levels off at a right-hand hairpin curve. Look for the blue-ribboned trail (Langdale Creek Waterfall trail) that joins in from the left (southerly). Follow the blue trail through the beautiful section of open forest. Keep a sharp lookout for the pink trail intersection uphill on the right. Follow the pink trail as it intersects and follows an old road leading steeply then more gradually uphill. Watch for a spur road on your right. Here the pink markers lead you temporarily downhill before rising sharply to the left at yet another intersection. The road is soon left behind as the trail leads northerly and crosses Hutchinson Creek. Climbing rapidly through a dark immature forest, you are soon brought to your destination—the summit—at the open rock outcrop.

If you have energy to spare, it is just a half-hour walk to the logging roads high up on Mount Elphinstone, but the connecting trail may be very rough and ill defined.

Langdale Creek Waterfall (Blue Markers)

Access: From Gibsons, take North Road to Stewart Road and go through the flashing light at the top of the bypass hill to where the road ends in a "T". Park and walk down the right-hand road for about 100 yards. Look for the

Howe Sound from Mt. Elphinstone.
The "drowned landscape" at its most ethereal.

trailhead on the left before the powerlines.

Hiking Time: 20 minutes up; 20 minutes down.

Description: Primary. The trail begins in a beautiful stand of tall second-growth timber. You should soon find a tree with four different-coloured aluminum markers indicating other trails. For the Langdale Creek Waterfall trail, follow the blue diamonds. The trail leads uphill along the edge of Langdale Creek ravine to an open area where you meet up with an old road you will follow. Soon after you re-enter the forest, bear right and, following the blue markers, leave the road behind. From this point the grade becomes slightly more challenging until the trail reaches the falls.

You may hear the waterfall long before you see it. Your first view of the falls is probably your best. The foolhardy may wish to explore the steep ravine—be very careful! Langdale Falls is actually a double waterfall, but from the trail only the upper section is visible. Should you wish to continue, the trail goes above the falls to a view south over Keats and Bowen islands.

Note: If the creek is very low, you can cross here and follow the blue then pink markers to K2 (see K2 hiking trail).

Tramway Trail (Red Markers)

This trail follows the route of two industrial tramways that took supplies to shake cutters working high on the mountain in the 1920s. The lower tramway, about 600 m (2,000 ft) long, lifted supplies to the Stoltz Company's First Camp, while the higher tramway carried supplies 1 km (.6 mi) farther uphill from First to Second Camp.

Access: From Gibsons, take North Road to Cemetery Road, then follow Cemetery for about one kilometre (.6 mi) to Keith Road, which may not be marked, but leads off to the right. Follow Keith for about one half kilometre (.3 mi) and look for the sign for Boothill Ranch. Turn left on the dirt road just before the ranch and follow it to the yellow gate. Park, walk through the gate and begin walking up the wide trail. just to the left of the old cemetery plots, look for the trailhead with the red diamond marker.

Hiking Time: Less than 30 minutes to First Camp. There are intersecting trails, so how long it takes to get back is largely up to you.

Description: Intermediate to advanced; easy to follow but steep. To the left of the trail near First Camp, you may see the lower tramway flywheel. To the right, look for the log frame of the tramway.

The trail continues and crosses the rock outcrop which forms the level site of First Camp. At its peak, First Camp was the hub of an operation involving three other camps: Japanese Camp, Chinese Camp and Second Camp. You may notice a trail on the right marked by white diamonds. This leads to the old Japanese Camp, roughly following the route of a flume and pack road.

First Camp is now largely a field of salmonberries. This site was the location of logging and sawmilling as early as 1903, when a company known as Drew-Battle built a log and earthfill dam to supply their steam-powered sawmill and flat-bottomed flume. Everything but the dam and remains of the iron boiler was destroyed by a huge fire in 1906.

Following the red trail across Chaster Creek, you can still see the remains of the dam. As Tramway Trail leaves First Camp, it crosses Chaster Creek, then winds to the right and passes the almost unnoticeable Chinese Camp skid road. The trail then crosses the upper tramway and turns uphill to follow it along its entire length.

The upper tramway is unique in that it rolled over round poles instead of square tracks. Consequently the wheels were concave, like giant clothesline pulleys. A few tracks can still be seen near the side of the trail as it nears its end at an old logging road. Please leave these artifacts as you found them. Following the more recent logging road allows you to ascend or descend by other trails.

BIKING TRAILS

Sprockids Mountain Bike Park
This is a series of approximately 14 km (8.4 mi) of trails that range in difficulty from beginner to expert. These trails are open to everyone and are a great place to go for a ride or a hike. The trails have been developed,

maintained and upgraded mostly by young volunteers and under the direction of Glen Illingworth, a dedicated mountain biker who is responsible for designing the majority of the trails in the park. The park is home to several major youth mountain bike championships, club rides and events. For further information, contact Doug Detwiller, phone/fax 886-0772.

Access: From the Langdale ferry terminal, follow the Gibsons Bypass straight up the hill. At the "T" (Stewart Road) turn right and then left at the "T". Follow the road to its end and park.

Elphinstone Bike Loop

This ride offers some great views of Howe Sound and its islands.

Access: Anywhere between Port Mellon and Roberts Creek.

Riding Time/Distance: 3 hours, 42 km (25.2 mi).

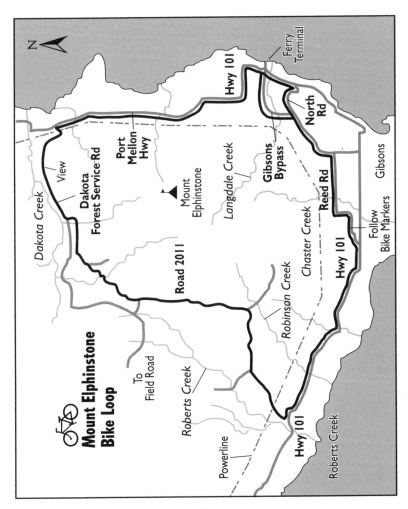

Description: Advanced (due to grade). Marked in both directions with the biking symbol or a double band of red paint. From the Langdale ferry terminal, turn right on the Port Mellon Highway. Carry on for 9 km (5.4 mi) to the Dakota Creek Forest Service Road. Turn left. The first 6.5 km (4 mi) are very steep. Don't be embarrassed if you have to get off and walk up some parts. After 4.2 km (2.5 mi) turn left on a road marked 2011, and stay on it 2.1 km (1.3 mi) later when it forks again. After another 3 km (1.8 mi) the road forks again. The right branch leads to Field Road. Stay on the left, up the steep hill, and then prepare for some good downhill to Roberts Creek and the Sunshine Coast Highway. Turn left at the highway and left again at Gibsons.

Hazards: There may be active logging on some of the roads, in which case they will be open to the public only on weekends.

KAYAKING HOWE SOUND

Howe Sound offers miles of protected waterways and clusters of islands. All the waterways are home to a wide variety of wildlife which the kayaker is in a unique position to observe. Study marine charts of the area to see the endless possibilities for exploring.

Access: Howe Sound can be accessed from Lower Gibsons at the government dock, or from a put-in just past the Gibsons Marina. From the Sunshine Coast Highway, stay on the main street of lower Gibsons as it curves around the waterfront until you reach Headlands Road and turn left to the water. Launch and then park on the road.

The Sound can also be accessed from the Port Mellon Highway. From the ferry terminal, turn right and drive about 10 km (6 mi) to a small settlement. Watch for an apartment block on your right, followed almost immediately by Dunham Road which leads to the water. Park well back because high tides come right up to the road.

Hazards: Howe Sound near Port Mellon is said to have the greatest concentration of log booms anywhere in the world. Tugs and deadheads are common here. Winds can also whistle through the narrow channels. High seas are rare, but winds can produce heavy chop.

The Sunshine Coast provides unlimited boating opportunities—whether you're sailing, motoring or travelling under your own steam.

The ferry from Horseshoe Bay takes the visitor through some of the world's most impressive scenery.

The wake from the ferry can also create problems.

This part of the Sunshine Coast encompasses the ferry lane to Horseshoe Bay, and there is also a great deal of commercial traffic. Consult charts for shipping lanes and steer well clear. If it is bigger than you, it has the right of way.

Points of Interest: Herons hang out on the log booms near Port Mellon; kingfishers and seals make this area their home.

Around Gambier Island, look for evidence of the island's logging past. In Collingwood Channel, watch for birds, seals and even the occasional whale. On the tiny islet just south of Anvil Island is the largest seal colony in the area. Look for cormorant nests on Anvil, structures two to three feet high on the rocky ledges.

Trips to Gambier Island

To Ekins Point: As little as 3 hours.

Thornbrough Bay and New Brighton: Crossing to the island takes about 30 minutes. Exploring can take as long as you like.

Halkett Bay Provincial Park: Four hours paddling to the park. This is a good weekend trip. Campsites are available.

Trips to Keats Island

To Plumper Cove: 3 hours.

Circumnavigation of Keats: 4 or 5 hours for the 12.8-km (7.5 mi) trip.

WHERE TO STAY IN & NEAR GIBSONS

Bonniebrook Lodge. Lodge, Bed and Breakfast, Campground, RV Park. 1532 Ocean Beach Esplanade, off Gower Point Road. Phone: 886-2887. Fax: 886-8853. Mailing address: RR #4, C 34, Gibsons, BC, V0N 1V0. Ocean front, non-smoking units; Chez Philippe restaurant; shaded campsites, fire pits, showers, toilets, laundry, picnic tables. Accepts major credit cards. Pets in campground only.

Bucktail Bed and Breakfast. 689 Winn Road, Box 531, Gibsons, V0N 1V0. Phone: 886-3610. Fax: 886-1357. On the Seawalk in Gibsons Harbour. Private moorage, gourmet breakfast, no credit cards, no pets.

Cedars Inn. Hotel. 895 Sunshine Coast Highway, Gibsons. Phone: 886-3008. Fax: 886-3046. Mailing address: Box 739, Gibsons, BC, V0N 1V0. TV, phones, coffee makers, pool, hot tub, sauna, mini-gym, restaurant, pub. Close to beaches and marinas. Accepts major credit cards. Pets accepted.

Irwin Motel. 826 Sunshine Coast Highway, Gibsons. Phone: 886-3331. Mailing address: RR #2, S 2, C 11, Gibsons, BC, V0N 1V0. TV, phones, kitchens. Near shopping and restaurants. Accepts major credit cards. Small pets accepted.

Langdale Heights RV Park. 2170 Port Mellon Highway, RR 6, Gibsons, V0N 1V0. Phone/fax: 886-2182, toll-free: 1-800-234-7138. We welcome families, small pets on leashes, tenters on our grassy open area. Breathtaking views, 9-hole golf course, 5 minutes from shopping and restaurants, large fully-serviced RV sites.

Marina House Bed and Breakfast. 846 Marine Drive, Gibsons V0N 1V0. Phone: 886-7888. A romantic, waterfront heritage home with charm, character and close to Gibsons Landing Marina and Molly's Reach. No pets.

Maritimer Bed and Breakfast. 521 South Fletcher, Box 256 Gibsons, V0N 1V0. Phone: 886-0664. Close to Molly's Reach and amenities. Large rooms, private entrances, decks, adult-oriented, non-smoking.

Ritz Motel. 505 Gower Point Road, Gibsons. Phone: 886-3343. Mailing address: Box 1022, Gibsons, BC, V0N 1V0. TV, phones, kitchenettes, laundry. Near restaurants, pubs, shopping, yacht club and marinas. Accepts major credit cards. Pets accepted.

Skyline Lodge Bed and Breakfast. 313 Skyline Drive, Box 486, Gibsons, V0N 1V0. Phone: 886-9160, toll-free 1-888-882-9160. Fax: 886-9196. Mediterranean-style villa. Picturesque view, spa room with hot tub, sauna, near restaurants and shopping, adult-oriented, no pets.

Sunnycrest Motel. 835 Sunshine Coast Highway, Gibsons. Phone: 886-2419. Fax: 886-7100. Mailing address: Box 856, Gibsons, BC, V0N 1V0. Some units have kitchens, all with complimentary coffee and tea. Near shopping centre, restaurants, pub and movie theatre. Accepts major credit cards. No pets.

DINING OUT IN GIBSONS

As prices change with the economy we have used $ signs to indicate relative prices.

$ means 2 people can eat, have a bottle of wine (if licensed) and get out for under $30 or so. $$ is $40–$50 and $$$ is over $50.

Chez Philippe Restaurant (at Bonniebrook Lodge), 1532 Ocean Beach Esplanade; 886-2188. French cuisine with West Coast flavour. Reservations recommended. $$$

Haus Uropa Restaurant, 426 Gower Point Road; 886-8326. European-style family dining. $$

Leo's Mediterranean Tapas and Grill, 274 Gower Point Road; 886-9414. Mediterranean cuisine. $

Molly's Reach, 647 School Road; 886-9710. Pizza, steak, seafood. $

Opa, 281 Gower Point Road; 886-4023. Japanese cuisine: sushi, tempura, sashimi, teriyaki. Take-out available. $$

Pack Rat Louie's Grill, 818 Gibsons Way; 886-1646. Pasta, seafood, desserts. $$

Bayview Gardens, 418 Marine Drive; 886-9219. Chinese cuisine. $$

Truffles, 264 Gower Point Road; 886-4545. Hearty soups and sandwiches, salads, desserts, cappuccino. $

Waterfront Restaurant, 440 Marine Drive; 886-2831. Overlooks the harbour. Steak, seafood. $$

GIBSONS TO ROBERTS CREEK

Roberts Creek: The Gumboot Nation

The Sunshine Coast Highway is both the bane and the life blood of the Sunshine Coast. In many places it is the only road from point A to point B and must be shared between vacationers with all the time in the world and frantic ferry-bound local traffic.

Narrow, winding, hilly and scenic though it is, there are other roads on the coast even more exotic, and by sticking to the main drag the visitor accidentally passes by some of the coast's hidden treasures—such as Roberts Creek (pop. 2,477), the next community north of Gibsons. For those not racing for a ferry, Lower Roberts Creek Road, accessed at either end from the Sunshine Coast Highway, provides a picturesque 8-km (5-mi) drive along the coast parallel to the highway.

Although there was some European settlement here before they arrived, the Roberts family gave the area its name. Thomas William (Will) Roberts immigrated from England in 1889 and pre-empted the quarter section near the mouth of the creek that now bears the family name.

Will's son Harry Roberts built the first store in the area in about 1908. Opening hours coincided with the arrival of the Union Steamship boats—or whenever a customer needed something. Harry is credited with giving the Sunshine Coast its name when he painted "Sunshine Belt" on his freight shed in the 1920s.

The Seaview Market was built in 1943 slightly upstream from Harry's enterprise. Although spiritually the same place, the "heart of downtown

*The Gumboot Garden Cafe, the heart
of the Gumboot Nation.*

Roberts Creek" was completely renovated a few years ago.

The entire Sunshine Coast became something of a haven for counter-culture citizens during the 1960s, but there was an extra concentration around Roberts Creek that is still reflected in the number of artisans, artists and craftspeople who live there.

Occasionally residents call their home-land The Independent Nation of Roberts Creek. The official footwear of the nation is the gumboot, a symbol proudly borne by the Gumboot Garden Cafe—a combination art gallery and funky restaurant.

The Community Hall—the workman-like building near the intersection of the Sunshine Coast Highway and Roberts Creek Road—may not look like much from outside or in, but it has deep roots in the community. A 1931 campaign to start a community centre failed to raise enough money, and the funds collected were returned to the donors. The following year, a more enthusiastic attempt began. The building was completed in 1934 on land donated by Harry Roberts.

A new complex in "downtown Roberts Creek," blends right into the old ambiance, housing more interesting shops and businesses.

There is a pleasant little park at the foot of Roberts Creek Road. You might still hear this general area called "the Propane Dock," an allusion to its many years as the site of a huge propane storage tank. It is also the site of Harry Roberts' store, sawmill and steamer dock.

For fine seafood in a beautiful building, try the Creekhouse, across from the General Store. There are many Bed and Breakfast establishments in Roberts Creek and the beautifully wooded Roberts Creek Provincial Park (and campground).

On the Sunshine Coast Highway above Roberts Creek, Cliff Gilker Park offers a nice introduction to the second growth coastal

BALD EAGLE

Few birds are as impressive as the bald eagle. In the spring, it can often be seen near the shore-line, hunting food for its voracious young. The adult has a chocolate-brown body (it often appears black), a white head and tail and a strong, hooked, golden-coloured bill.

Bald eagles' distinctive stick nests are built in tall trees, giving them a springboard from which to search for prey. Eagles are experts at catching thermals, flapping their wings only to change direction. From the ground, they can easily be confused with vultures, the major difference being that eagles' wings are straight, while vultures soar with their wings in a V-shape. Adult bald eagles have white only on the head and tail. Vultures have light patches when seen from below.

forest and the Sunshine Coast Golf and Country Club offers a full range of facilities immediately next door.

Roberts Creek has some of the only sandy beaches on the mainland part of the lower Sunshine Coast. McFarlane's beach at the creek mouth is a sweeping crescent of soft sand. Roberts Creek Park at the foot of Flume Road also has sand intermingled with wave-smoothed bedrock.

From Roberts Creek, it is about a 10- to 15-minute drive along the Sunshine Coast Highway to Sechelt, the next community north.

Cliff Gilker Park

This park lacks only seafront to make it a perfectly representative west coast habitat. Here you will find hiking trails, picnic facilities, baseball diamonds and several waterfalls. In April, it hosts local Earth Day festivities.

Access: Approximately 11 km (6.5 mi) north of Gibsons (measuring from Sunnycrest Mall) and adjacent to the Sunshine Coast Golf Course. Follow the signs.

BIKING TRAILS IN THE ROBERTS CREEK AREA

Roberts Creek Bike Loop

This bike loop is steep but offers great views of the Tetrahedron Range and the Strait of Georgia. You can also access several other nearby trails.

Access: From Gibsons, head north along the Sunshine Coast Highway 10 km (6 mi) and turn right on the Roberts Creek Forest Service Road. If you come to Cliff Gilker Park, you have gone too far by 500 m (.3 mi). Head up the Forest Service road for 1 km (.6 mi) and park at the powerline.

Time/Distance: 2 hours, 30 km (18 mi).

Description: Intermediate to advanced. The route is marked counter-clockwise with the biking symbol or a double band of orange paint. It is steep, with a total climb of 800 m (.5 mi). Stay on the main fork of the Forest Service road at the intersection 4.5 km (2.7 mi) from the start. The other fork leads to a viewpoint about 1 km (.6 mi) away. You will come to another inter-section 4 km (2.4 mi) farther on. Bear left. The other fork is the beginning of the Dakota Creek Loop. Keep on the main road 13 km (8 mi). Take Field Road back to the highway and turn left to return to the Roberts Creek Forest Service Road.

Clack Creek Bike Loop

This route offers great downhill! The Brodie Trail follows it in places. (See map on page 46).

Access: From Sunshine Coast Highway, 10 km (6 mi) north of Gibsons, turn right on the Roberts Creek Forest Service Road. If you come to Cliff Gilker Park, you have gone too far by 500 m (.3 mi). Follow the Forest Service road until it turns into Lockyer Road and continue 2 km (1.2 mi) to Gruman Road. Park.

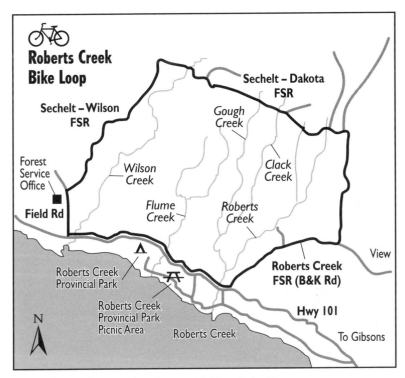

Roberts Creek
Bike Loop

Sechelt – Dakota FSR

Sechelt – Wilson FSR

Gough Creek

Forest Service Office

Wilson Creek

Clack Creek

Field Rd

Flume Creek

Roberts Creek

View

Roberts Creek Provincial Park

Roberts Creek FSR (B&K Rd)

Roberts Creek Provincial Park Picnic Area

Hwy 101

N

Roberts Creek

To Gibsons

Time/Distance: 45 minutes, 12.3 km (7.4 mi).

Description: Intermediate. Marked counterclockwise with the biking symbol or a double band of yellow paint. Head right, along Gruman Road. At 500 m (.3 mi) you may elect to take the old skid road off into the bushes—be warned that it is overgrown and steep. You can stay on Gruman for another 1.8 km (1.1 mi), then turn left on Clack Creek Forest Service Road. Follow the road for 5 km (3.1 mi). Here the road ends. Take the old skid road (described as "exhilarating" by some) for 2 km (1.2 mi) downhill where you will intersect the East Wilson Forest Service Road. Turn left and follow the road back to the start, about 2 km (1.2 mi).

Brodie Trails Bike Loop

This is the Brodie Test of Metal '93 Mountain Bike race course. (See map on page 47.)

Access: From Sunshine Coast Highway, 10 km (6 mi) north of Gibsons, turn right on the Roberts Creek Forest Service Road. If you come to Cliff Gilker Park, you have gone too far by 500 m (.3 mi). Head 1 km (.6 mi) up the Forest Service road to the powerlines and park.

Time/Distance: 40 minutes, 7.5 km (4.5 mi).

Description: Intermediate to advanced. The route is marked clockwise with the biking symbol, or a double band of orange paint and the letter

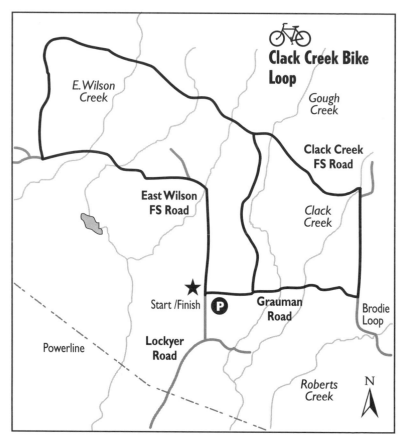

"B." Head north (left) under the powerline and turn right into the bush after 450 m (.3 mi). Cross the creek and carry on for 800 m (.5 mi) and turn right. Climb for about 1.4 km (.8 mi) and turn right on the logging road. Take this to the next junction and turn left on the main line. Follow the main line for 500 m (.3 mi) and turn right into the bush. Keep right on this downhill and back to the powerline. Turn right and follow the powerline back to where you started.

WHERE TO STAY IN ROBERTS CREEK

Country Cottage Bed and Breakfast. 1183 Roberts Creek Road, Box 183, Roberts Creek, V0N 2W0. Phone: 885-7448. Idyllic sheep farm, near beach, flyfishing, kayaking, back-country skiing, adult oriented, no credit cards.

Moon Cradle Backpackers Retreat. 3125 Sunshine Coast Highway (101). Phone: 885-2070. Hostel-style B&B on 5 acres. Ten minute walk to beach.

Roberts Creek Provincial Park & Campground. Sunshine Coast

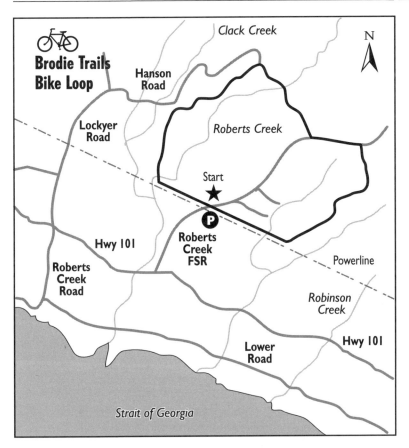

Highway, Roberts Creek. Phone: (604) 898-3678. Mailing address: Box 220, Brackendale, BC, V0N 1H0. Open May to September. Large wooded site, beach access. Sani-station nearby. No credit cards. Pets must be leashed.

Rosewood Bed and Breakfast. 575 Pine Road, Gibsons (on the boundary with Roberts Creek). Phone: 886-4714. Mailing address: RR #2, S 46, C 21, Gibsons, BC, V0N 1V0. Feature room has private entrance, queen bed, fireplace. Reservations recommended. No credit cards. No pets.

Welcome Inn Bed and Breakfast. 1176 Flume Road, General Delivery, Roberts Creek, V0N 2W0. Phone: 740-0318, toll-free: 1-800-986-0001. Fax: 604 740-0318. Heritage-style home; near beach, golf, store, no pets.

Willows Inn Bed & Breakfast Cottage. 3440 Beach Ave, Box 1036, Sechelt, V0N 3A0. Phone 885-2452, toll-free: 1-877-885-5559. Fax: 604 885-5872. Detached cottage, near beach, non smoking, no pets.

*The "propane dock" at Roberts Creek
is now a family park.*

DINING OUT IN ROBERTS CREEK

As prices change with the economy we have used $ signs to indicate relative prices.

$ means 2 people can eat, have a bottle of wine (if licensed) and get out for under $30 or so. $$ is $40–$50 and $$$ is over $50.

From the sophisticated elegance of the Creek House to the funky informality of the Gumboot Garden the dining-out possibilities in the Creek are ... well, that covers them. There's just the two, each one excellent in its own way.

Creekhouse Restaurant, 1041 Roberts Creek Road; 885-9321. Fine dining. Reservations recommended. $$$.

The Gumboot Garden, 1057 Roberts Creek Road; 885-4216. Vegetarian dishes. No credit cards. $$.

But don't forget the picnic possibilities:

Roberts Creek Provincial Park Picnic Ground, End of Flume Road.

The **Pier at the end of Roberts Creek Road** has been renovated and is now a picnic ground complete with tables, barbecues and a beach trail.

Cliff Gilker Park, Sunshine Coast Highway.

THE DISTRICT OF SECHELT

Continuing north along the Sunshine Coast Highway from Roberts Creek, the highway is lined with tall trees. Douglas fir and red cedar were once the economic life blood of the coast. Almost all the area has been logged and burned off, yet in a relatively short time the trees have grown back so vigorously that you can almost forget how close you are to the sea.

A shopping centre marks the community of Wilson Creek. On the left, towards the water, is a huge condominium and marina development. To the right, up Field Road, are the Chapman Creek fish hatchery, many of the area's light industries, the Forest Service offices, and the Sechelt airport.

As you sweep around the curve that brings you into Sechelt, at Davis Bay, there is no forgetting. You come across a seascape prospect all the more amazing for being visible so suddenly. You will probably want to pull up and park.

The dock at Davis Bay.
A surprising number of salmon are caught here.

Here is a view that takes in the Sunshine Coast itself as far as the Trail Islands (the nearest group of forested islands) and beyond. Across the Strait of Georgia, you can see Mount Washington, Nanaimo and other communities on Vancouver Island. Immediately offshore are the White Islets—low rocky outcroppings that derive their name from the decorative by-products of the thousands of sea gulls that roost there. The view south takes in Vancouver, and occasionally Mount Baker in Washington state.

Here there are several restaurants and a drive-in where you can find seafood, burgers and fine dining, and arguably the best fish'n'chips on the coast.

There are two motels right across the road from the beach—one of the

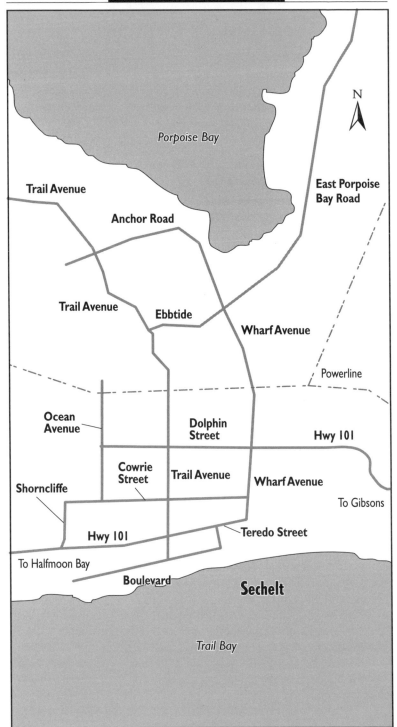

The beach in Sechelt—it's all rocks now but rumour has it that the sand was all hauled away to Vancouver beaches in the last century.

few easily accessible beaches on the Sunshine Coast. Though there is no life-guard, it is still a safe place for kids to play while parents lounge on the logs or join in the fun. Fishermen can try their luck from the prominent pier.

As we were preparing the revisions to this edition of *Sunshine and Salt Air*, traffic at the "entry" to Sechelt was chaotic. The road was being widened to accommodate a new shopping mall under construction near the hospital. We hope by the time you arrive all will be resolved. The traffic light at the main intersection at Wharf Road marks the centre of the lower Sunshine Coast. Many of our mileage measurements are taken from this point.

A right turn takes you to Porpoise Bay on Sechelt Inlet where there is a government wharf and launching ramp, a marina, the Lighthouse Pub and Keeper's restaurant.

Continue up Sechelt Inlet Road to Porpoise Bay Provincial Park, one of the best camping deals around, situated near another easily accessible sandy beach. Look for nature programs in the summer and early fall, from sea life identification to salmon spawning in Angus Creek. Part of the campground is set aside especially for cyclists.

Sechelt Inlet Road also provides access to the 6,000-hectare (15,000-acre) Tetrahedron Recreation Area.

From Sechelt's main traffic light, a left turn takes you to restaurants and shops, where you can find everything from fishing and hunting gear to souvenirs and antiques.

Remember to check out the Arts Centre to see the works of the best local and national artists.

Plan to attend the Festival of the Written Arts and the accompanying Craft Fair if you are here in August.

As you drive out of Sechelt, don't miss the Wakefield Inn. A heritage log building festooned with logging mementos and photos, it is a great place for lunch. It also features live entertainment Thursday through Saturday evenings.

Like the other communities on the Sunshine Coast, Sechelt has a past that is linked with the ocean. When in 1895 the Whitaker family established Sechelt Townsite, straddling the isthmus which separates Trail Bay from the Sechelt Inlet, it could only be reached by water. By 1904 the family was promoting Sechelt as a "fashionable seaside resort," and had established wharves at Porpoise Bay and Trail Bay.

To accommodate freight shipments across the isthmus, the first road in the community, now Wharf Road, was built at a cost to the provincial treasury of $87.50, and another road was constructed to connect the Sechelt Indian lands to the town centre near the beach. Logging operations were well established in the inlet, and loggers mingled with tourists at the Beach House Hotel, which boasted a "very fine bar" and tearoom. Following a fire in 1914, the hotel was reconstructed approximately where the Driftwood Inn is located today.

The Union Steamship Company ran excursions to the resorts in Sechelt and Selma Park and built cottages along the waterfront in both

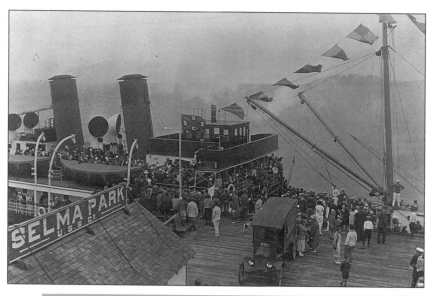

Meeting the steamer. The vintage truck on the landing should help you pin down the date.

locations. These excursions continued until the company ceased operations in the 1950s.

Until the late 1940s, commercial activity centred around Trail Bay, with its pavilion and steamship wharf, but by 1952, after the highway through town was paved, businesses began moving to Cowrie Street. "The community which was founded on access by sea was restructuring itself to access by road," says Helen Dawe in her definitive history of Sechelt. The wharf that had brought so many visitors to the area was destroyed by fire in 1963, as was the second Beach House Hotel.

In 1986, the village, which had clustered around the isthmus, expanded to fill the area from Davis Bay to West Sechelt.

The District of Sechelt includes Davis Bay, Wilson Creek, Selma Park, Sandy Hook, Tillicum Bay, Tuwanek and West Sechelt as well as Sechelt Village and several smaller neighbourhoods. Its population in the late 1990s was 6,843.

The local travel information centre is located in the Trail Bay Mall. Phone (604) 885-3100, fax 885-9538; write c/o Box 360, Sechelt, BC, V0N 3A0.

The Festival of the Written Arts

One of the premier cultural events on the Sunshine Coast is the annual Festival of the Written Arts, which brings together the cream of Canada's writers for a weekend of readings each August. Since its inception in 1983, the Festival has showcased such well-known personalities as Peter Gzowski, Mordecai Richler, Allan Fotheringham and W.P. Kinsella, to name only a few. The festival is always organized with careful attention to a balance of well-known names and future writing stars, and includes writers from the Sunshine Coast such as Anne Cameron, Edith Iglauer, Joni Mitchell, and Howard White.

The festival is held amid the spectacular gardens at Rockwood Centre in Sechelt. Readings take place at the Pavilion, built specially

Rockwood Lodge in Sechelt—home of the Festival of the Written Arts.

for the festival, while the other two buildings house a festival bookshop and a refreshment area.

Subscription tickets go on sale in the spring and are available for the whole festival or for selected performances only. Events featuring the best-known writers tend to sell out quickly, so it is wise to purchase tickets well

PACIFIC DOGWOOD

The Pacific dogwood (*Cornus nuttallii*) is at its best from April to June when it flowers. The distinctive cream blossom, the official flower of BC, is in fact the bract; the flowers are minute purple or green blooms in the centre. The distinctive leaves are glossy dark green above and much lighter below, usually 7.5–10 cm (3–4 in) long with veins curving parallel to the leaf edge. The name is derived from the fact that skewers or "dags" were once made from the wood, hence "dagwood" and later dogwood.

The tree usually grows to 6–10 m (20–30 ft) in height, and to a diameter of 15–30 cm (6–12 in). While it grows all over the Coast, it is most noticeable along the Sunshine Coast Highway north of Halfmoon Bay. When not in flower, it tends to blend into the deciduous landscape. There may a second bloom in the late summer/early fall. The tree is protected by law and must not be disturbed.

Common lore says that Jesus' cross was made from dogwood, but God changed the form of the tree so that it would never be used for such a purpose again.

in advance. If you can't do so, check with the box office—some tickets will be available on performance days.

In conjunction with the festival, the Sunshine Coast Arts Council holds its annual summer craft sale at Hackett Park, near the Rockwood Centre. Many local artisans and craftspeople are showcased, and the sale's success and its reputation for quality attracts more and more artisans every year.

To get on the mailing list or for further information, visit the Writers' Festival office on the Rockwood grounds at the top of Cowrie Street in Sechelt, call (604) 885-9631, (fax 885-3967), or write Box 2299, Sechelt, BC, V0N 3A0.

Rockwood Centre

Rockwood Lodge, the imposing buildings at the top of Cowrie Street, might be called "the grand old lady" of the Sunshine Coast arts community. It is the headquarters of the Festival of the Written Arts, and the site of many other events throughout the year.

Built as a hotel in 1926 by William and Jessie Youngson, Rockwood earned the nickname "Government House" because of the large numbers of government officials who stayed there during the 10 years the couple operated it. Ownership had changed hands six times by 1980, when it was purchased by the Sechelt Chamber of Commerce; in 1984 it was leased to Western Moorbad Resort in an attempt to introduce coast folk to the delights of German-style mud-bathing. The venture failed in 1986, and the District of

Sechelt assumed the mortgage and gave a local group permission to manage the buildings (which now included a "North Wing" with 12 sleeping rooms) for community activities.

The original building was restored, the North Wing refurbished and the original landscaping upgraded to include the rhododendron gardens which are a highlight of any visitor's tour of the area. It was also designated a heritage site. The Festival of the Written Arts added the open-air pavilion where Canadian writers present their works every August.

Today the original hotel, the North Wing and the pavilion are home to meetings, seminars, workshops and recreational activities throughout the year.

Sunshine Coast Arts Centre

This unique log structure, at Trail and Medusa in Sechelt, is regarded as the core of artistic activity on the Sunshine Coast. The materials used in the building reflect its natural environment.

The first stage of the building was complete in 1978, bringing to fruition years of effort and dreaming by countless volunteers. More performance and studio space has since been added.

Displays at the Centre change frequently, presenting a goodly mix of solo and group shows by members of the Coast's artistic community and artists from off the coast. The Centre also hosts regular performing arts events, readings and courses.

The Arts Centre is open from Wednesday to Saturday from 11:00 a.m. to 4:00 p.m. and Sunday from 1:00 to 4:00 p.m. During the summer the hours are extended from 10:00 a.m. to 4:00 p.m. Tuesday to Saturday, 1:00 to 4:00 p.m. Sunday.

Some of the Sechelt Band's fine collection of totem poles.

The First Peoples of the Lower Sunshine Coast

For as long as the Sunshine Coast has been habitable, it has been home to First Nations people of the Coast Salish family. On the lower coast there were two main groups. A small group of the Squamish tribe of Howe Sound occupied the Gibsons area while the Sechelt Peninsula, Sechelt Inlet and Jervis Inlet areas were the home of the Sechelt nation. Sub-groups of the Sechelt were centred at the head of Jervis Inlet (the Hunaechin), in Deserted Bay (the Tsonai), in Pender Harbour (the Skaiakos) and in Sechelt Inlet (the Tuwanek).

The Sechelt people reached a significant turning point in their history in 1862 when the great smallpox epidemic reduced their numbers from many thousands to a few hundred. The survivors turned to Catholic missionaries of the Oblate order for help, and Father Paul Durieu moved them to a central mission at Chatalech, the site of present-day Sechelt. Under Durieu's autocratic "system" the Sechelt created a neat European-style village and became known as a progressive people.

In 1986, the Sechelt Band was the first in Canada to achieve self-government, allowing it to make decisions on land acquisition and disposal, borrowing, municipal zoning, education and welfare.

In May 1991, the House of Hewhiwus (House of Chiefs) on the Sunshine Coast Highway was dedicated. As well as housing the band administrative offices, gift shops, offices and a training centre, it is also the home of the Raven's Cry Theatre and tems swíya museum, which is a "must see" for visitors to the area. Band elders are vigorously striving to re-establish the language, history and traditions of the Sechelt people.

The Wakefield Inn

While enjoying lunch, dinner, hard-hitting music or a quiet pint at the Wakefield—or just admiring the view of the Trail Islands and Georgia Strait—you might not realize you are sitting in a historical building (photo pg 70).

The Wakefield dates from the late 1920s when it was built for Major Sutherland of the Provincial Police—probably by Hector MacDonald, a long-time resident who built several other similar log structures on the Sunshine Coast. The "Wakey" became a roadhouse pub in 1940, passing through the hands of various owners until the Radymski family bought it in the early 1970s. Although changes have been made from time to time, the overall integrity of the original building remains, and the walls are hung with photos and implements from the early days of logging.

BEACHES NEAR SECHELT

Davis Bay: Located on the highway north of Wilson Creek and south of Sechelt's town centre, this is one of the best and most accessible beaches on the coast. On a summer day as the tide comes in over the sand, the ocean water warms, making for pleasant swimming. The beach at Davis Bay is a great place for kite-flying and has been the home of a major sand castle competition in the summer. Dates are variable because of the tides. Davis Bay is also a haven for windsurfers because of its accessibility and dependable winds. Around the corner from the beach is the mouth of Chapman Creek, where in the fall salmon head upstream to spawn and a great variety of birds congregate.

Sechelt Town Centre Beaches: One of the area's most cherished legends is that the sandy beach that once graced the shores of Sechelt's town centre was taken away on barges and used to build up the beaches in Vancouver some time in the late nineteenth century. Most of the earliest photographs of

The coast's beaches aren't always this deserted,
but sometimes you can have one all to yourself.

the beach at Sechelt clearly show gravel, but some of them seem to picture sand. Could the photos merely be out of focus? There was a gravel operation on Sechelt's waterfront in the early part of this century. It certainly is a gravel beach now, but there are lots of logs that lend themselves to comfortable beach lounging. Wharf Street, Trail Avenue and Inlet Avenue all lead down to this beach.

Porpoise Bay Provincial Park: In addition to excellent camping and picnicking facilities, the park has a sandy beach fronting the protected waters of Sechelt Inlet.

To get there, turn east (away from the ocean) onto Wharf Road at the main traffic light in Sechelt. A few blocks later, turn right on Porpoise Bay Road, which shortly becomes Sechelt Inlet Road, and follow the signs about 4 km (2.5 mi) to the Provincial Park.

Mason Road Beach Access: Beach access can also be found at the foot of Mason Road, beside the Wakefield Inn, 3.5 km (2.1 mi) north of the Sechelt town centre on the Sunshine Coast Highway.

Wildlife Abounds at the Sechelt Marsh

The Sechelt marsh offers a small sanctuary and breeding ground for waterfowl within the township and a pleasant spot to view a variety of wild and liberated domestic waterfowl. The marsh was originally a beaver pond, but there have been no beaver sightings here recently.

To get there, turn away from the ocean onto Wharf Road at the traffic light in Sechelt. The marsh is on the left side of the road just short of Porpoise Bay.

Look for buffleheads, redwing blackbirds, Canada geese and mallards, h dearly love tourists and stir up V-shaped wakes racing toward any visitors they suspect of maybe carrying bags of goodies.

A little farther along Wharf Road is Porpoise Bay. The Lighthouse Pub and Keeper's Restaurant are popular establishments, and down on the government wharf, fresh-caught crabs and other seafoods are frequently for sale.

Kinnikinnick Park

This amazing park is in Sechelt, near the arena and a golf course, yet it is deserted most of the time.

You can spend anywhere from a few minutes to a few hours here. There are several trails, all well laid out, all easy. The worst things you'll run into here are mud in spring, and territorial Douglas squirrels.

Look for lots of representative plants here: skunk cabbage, star flower in June, bleeding hearts (floral, not political) and of course Kinnikinnick, the sprawling low-growing evergreen shrub that produces little pink flowers in spring and bright red berries later in the season.

To get there if you're coming into town along the highway from points south, drive straight ahead at the main traffic light in Sechelt. The street becomes Dolphin. Two blocks along, turn right on Trail Avenue. Follow the signs to the arena (Trail turns into Reef Road which eventually turns sharp left and becomes Shoal Way). Just past the arena on Shoal Way, look for the park entrance.

KINNIKINNICK

Kinnikinnick (*Arctostaphylos uva-ursi*) is a low-growing shrub which takes its name from a Native word for "smoking mixture." Also known as bear berry, its bright red berries can be eaten raw. In spring, it has small, pink, bell-shaped flowers. In Sechelt, it is so abundant that a park is named for it.

HIKING IN THE SECHELT AREA

Chapman Creek Hiking-Biking Trail

This hike-bike trail offers enough variety and interesting features to entertain the whole family, the avid hiker and the casual walker. The trail follows Chapman Creek and there are many points where you can access the creek for splashing and wading. In November and December, visitors can also see chum and coho salmon on their way upstream to spawn.

A real treat for young and old was added in 1996. Terry Chapman (no relation), a carver, created a series of gnomes and trolls along the trail. Artfully using the natural contours and configurations of old stumps and deadfalls, Chapman's creations blend in so well they were hard to spot even when brand new. In a few years' time they will look like they were always there. A symbol carved into a stump at the edge of the trail indicates that one of the faces is viewable from the spot—even so, you'll miss some of them. Just to keep it interesting, we're not going to tell you how many there are. More of Chapman's forest figures may be seen along the Klein-Ruby Lake Trail described in the Egmont section of this book.

Access: The trail begins in Brookman Park, located alongside the Sunshine Coast Highway next to the bridge across Chapman Creek in Davis Bay.

Hiking Time: 1 hour each way if you go all the way to the falls.

Description: Easy. The well-worn trail follows the creek upstream. The gnomes and trolls can be seen during the first half-hour of the trail. If you climb a very steep stairway from the creek, the trail joins another trail that leads to the right up the creek to the falls, and to the left to Selma Park and Davis Bay.

For bikers, the trail is rated as moderate to difficult. There is a steep hill in the middle of this one and some tricky technical sections beside the creek.

Hazards: No danger, but extremely muddy in season. Kids and dogs should be careful around the creek, which picks up quite a current following heavy rain and during spring run-off.

**The Chapman Creek Valley
unfolds in the mountains behind Sechelt.**

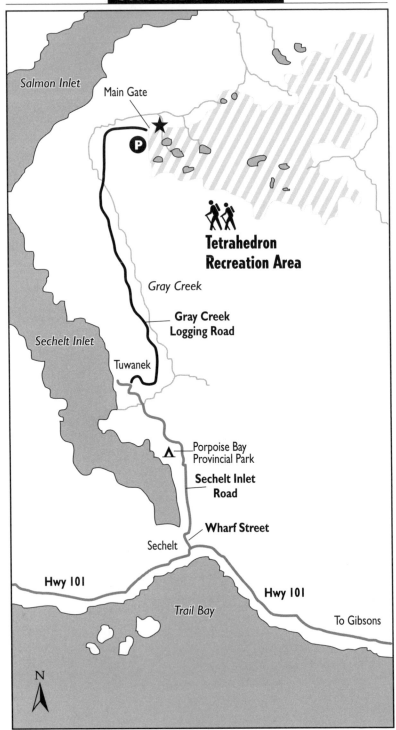

Salmon Inlet

Main Gate

P

Tetrahedron
Recreation Area

Gray Creek

**Gray Creek
Logging Road**

Sechelt Inlet

Tuwanek

Porpoise Bay
Provincial Park

**Sechelt Inlet
Road**

Wharf Street

Sechelt

Hwy 101

Hwy 101

Trail Bay

To Gibsons

N

Tetrahedron—The Sunshine Coast's Biggest and Newest Park

The 6,000-hectare (15,000-acre) Tetrahedron Recreation Area was proclaimed a Class A Provincial Park in 1995. This spectacular wilderness area is located in the mountains to the northeast of Sechelt. It ranges in elevation from 900 to 1,800 m (3,000–5,900') above sea level and includes mountains, old-growth forest, open parkland, 9 lakes and a variety of streams and wetlands. It also contains an extensive hiking and cross-country ski trail network that includes a great cabin-to-cabin (4 cabins) backcountry system in BC's Coast Mountains. The area is home to bear, cougar, marmots, mountain goat and deer. The area also feeds the headwaters of Chapman and Gray creeks, which provide drinking water to parts of the Sunshine Coast. For the latest information on the park, contact BC Parks at (604) 898-3678. Pets are not allowed in the park.

Access: Before planning a trip to this park, be sure to call Fleetwood Forest Products at (604) 885-4027 to determine if there are logging trucks using the road. Access may be limited to weekends only.

From the main traffic lights in Sechelt, turn east (inland) onto Wharf Road. A few blocks later, turn right on Porpoise Bay Road, which shortly becomes Sechelt Inlet Road, and follow it 5 km (3 mi) past Porpoise Bay Provincial Park to Gray Creek Forest Service Road.

Turn right and follow the logging road 12.3 km (7.4 mi) to the parking area. Be sure to keep left at the Y-intersection about 1.6 km (1 mi) from the start.

The parking area is accessible by family car in the summer, but it is four-wheel drive country in winter. Winter users should carry chains, as only limited plowing is done.

Don't do this, don't do that: Because of its relative isolation and because the area forms part of the Coast's watershed, everyone using the area is asked to observe a few rules:

Don't waste firewood. Although the cabins are offered free on a first-come, first-serve basis, anyone using the cabins or camping in the vicinity is asked to be very conservative with the firewood, which is supplied by the Tet Ski Club in co-operation with International Forest Products, Fleetwood Logging and BC Parks, and must be airlifted to the cabins. As well, don't burn outdoor fires which waste wood and leave unsightly debris. Backpack stoves should be used for cooking.

Don't erect a tent on any ecologically sensitive area, including the heather which grows at higher elevations.

Don't leave garbage behind. Practise "no trace" camping. The cabins and surroundings are maintained by the ski club on a volunteer basis.

Don't do anything which might damage the water source.

Hazards: This is an upper elevation back country area. Be prepared to wait out storms. Cross-country skiers are advised that the terrain is intermediate to advanced with variable terrain. You must be experienced to assess the risks here.

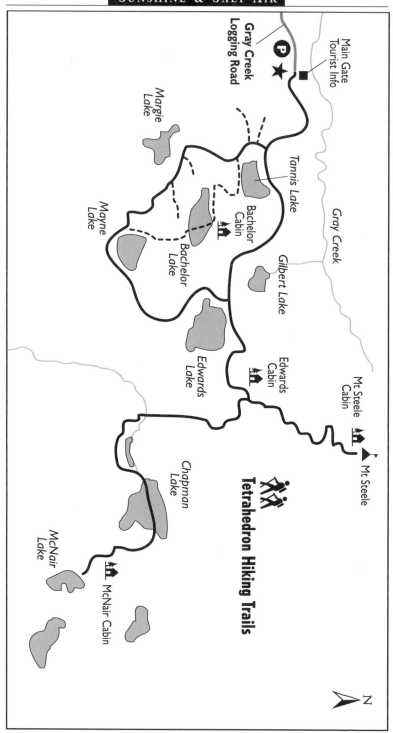

*BC's newest park, Tetrahedron
and the mountain for which it is named.*

BIKING IN THE SECHELT AREA

Angus Creek Bike Loop

This bike loop offers amazing views of Sechelt Inlet, Mount Richardson, the Caren Range Plateau and Sechelt. (See map on page 64.)

Access: Start in Sechelt on your bike, or drive to Porpoise Bay Provincial Park to begin. To get to the park, turn east (inland) onto Wharf Road at the main traffic light in Sechelt. Three blocks later, turn right on Porpoise Bay Road, which shortly becomes Sechelt Inlet Road, and follow the signs about 4 km (2.5 mi) to the park.

Time/Distance: 1.5 hours, 22 km (13.2 mi.)

Description: Intermediate. If you rode your bike from Sechelt, turn east (right) at the Sechelt-Crucil Forest Service Road (AKA the Sechelt landfill road). If you drove to the park, backtrack on your bike toward Sechelt for 3 km (1.8 mi), then turn east (left) onto the same Forest Service road.

The loop actually begins here and is marked counterclockwise with the biking symbol or a double band of orange paint. Parts of the first section are very steep. Ride 4 km (2.4 mi) up the Forest Service road, past the landfill. When you come to a major junction, keep left. Follow the main branch for 7.5 km (4.5 mi). Descend to the Gray Creek crossing and take the main branch back to Sechelt Inlet Road. Turn left and head back toward Porpoise Bay Park or Sechelt.

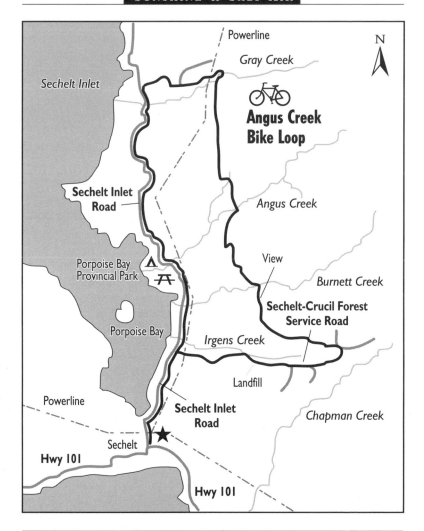

Powerline
Gray Creek
N

Sechelt Inlet

Angus Creek
Bike Loop

Sechelt Inlet
Road

Angus Creek

Porpoise Bay
Provincial Park

View

Burnett Creek

Sechelt-Crucil Forest
Service Road

Porpoise Bay

Irgens Creek

Landfill

Powerline

Sechelt Inlet
Road

Chapman Creek

Sechelt

Hwy 101

Hwy 101

CANOEING AND KAYAKING SECHELT INLET

Sechelt Inlet and its associated inlets (Salmon and Narrows) provide some delightful paddling experiences. Sheltered from the big seas of the Strait of Georgia by the surrounding hills and free from any severe tidal currents, this inland sea offers a wide variety of options for paddlers of all skill levels, whether you are spending an afternoon or staying for a week.

Among the attractions are 8 marine park sites, where development is limited to sanitary facilities and rustic campgrounds. Some of the 8 sites, however, are completely undeveloped. There is also camping, a broad sand beach and a grassy picnic area at Porpoise Bay Provincial Park.

On the west shore of the inlet, the rocks and mud flats are home to a variety of marine life. The eelgrass is a favoured hangout for crabs. Around Poise Island, look for giant Sunflower starfish.

Tuwanek Point Marine Park offers a great beach, perfect for swimming and walking. Just south of Nine Mile Point, look for pictographs in red ochre on the cliff 3–5 m (10–15 ft) above the high-tide mark. These are good examples of the many pictographs all over the Sunshine Coast. Nine Mile Point has another marine park with a small beach.

At Kunechin Point, you will probably encounter dive boats, as this is the resting place of the *Chaudiere,* a destroyer sunk by the Artificial Reef Society to create a dive site that is now the most popular on the Sunshine Coast, and one of the most popular in North America. The marine park at the point offers campsites and sanitary facilities, but no reliable fresh water supply. In the spring, the area draws seals to feast on the fish that congregate here.

Behind Halfway Island lies Halfway Beach, which has fine camping areas, although no water is available. Seals congregate on the island.

At the mouth of Narrows Inlet is Storm Bay. In the 1960s, this was a favourite spot for "flower children" to set up housekeeping, and the structures in the bay reflect its past.

Tzoonie Narrows, the "pinch" in the middle of Narrows Inlet, can create a current of 3 knots at full tidal flow. It is noticeable when you work against it and great fun when you go with it, so plan your day accordingly if you can. Camping is available on the east side of the narrows. Narrows Inlet is ideal for family activities as it is well protected, features beaches for kids and hikes in the surrounding hills.

Access: There are 5 good launch sites in the Inlet. The one nearest to Sechelt is at the head of Porpoise Bay. Turn east (inland)

GREAT BLUE HERON

The great blue heron, a study in contrasts, is an unofficial symbol of the Sunshine Coast. As it solemnly examines tidal pools or picks its way along the beach, it is a picture of grace and beauty. When it takes flight, giving its raucous cry, its legs splayed behind it, or when it lands on a precarious perch, it is a study in clumsiness.

A large bird with graceful blue-grey plumes, the heron has a wingspan that can reach 1.2 m (4 ft). It searches for fish in tidal pools, and gives rise to the saying: "As hopeful as a heron at a bait dock" as it stalks piers and docks.

The heron is common everywhere along the shores of the Sunshine Coast.

onto Wharf Road at the main traffic lights in Sechelt and follow Wharf to the government dock and Lighthouse Pub. A public boat ramp is directly to the left of the pub. There is plenty of parking near the head of the dock. If you plan to leave your vehicle there for more than three days, please advise the wharf manager (885-1986).

Another launch site is located 4 km (2.4 mi) down the east side of the inlet at the Porpoise Bay Provincial Park. To get there, turn east (inland) onto Wharf Road at the main traffic lights in Sechelt. Three blocks later, turn right on Porpoise Bay Road, which shortly becomes Sechelt Inlet Road, and follow the signs to the park.

The third launch site is at Sandy Hook. Follow Sechelt Inlet Road 3.2 km (2 mi) past the entrance to Porpoise Bay Provincial Park. Turn left at Sandy Hook Road and wind your way down to the small park and launch area.

The fourth option is to follow Sechelt Inlet Road about 1.6 km (1 mi) past Sandy Hook Road to Naylor Road and look for the Tillicum Marina sign where launch facilities and parking are available.

The final put-in site is at Tuwanek, where a small spit reaches out toward the Lamb Islets. Keep to the left at the "Y" junction just past the Jackson dry land sort. Be aware that this is a popular spot for divers as well, and parking is very limited.

Hazards: Near Porpoise Bay, kayakers will encounter commercial and private craft as well as seaplanes.

Winds in the mid-afternoon can be strong, especially in summer, but high seas are rare. The winds can be variable because of the inlet's configuration. In high winds, the western shore offers most protection.

The mouth of Salmon Inlet can be hazardous as the winds of the two inlets generate confused waters, and there are few landing beaches up Salmon Inlet.

Bears inhabit the area around Kunechin Point. Take the appropriate precautions.

At the head of the inlet is Skookumchuck Narrows (Sechelt Rapids). During large tides, the current can run as fast as 14 knots and whirlpools can easily overwhelm small boats. Keep well clear of this area. It is very dangerous!

Trips: Porpoise Bay to Snake Bay to Four Mile Point and back to the dock, 4 to 5 hours.

Tuwanek to Nine Mile Point. Launch at Tuwanek, paddle to Nine Mile Point and back, 4 to 5 hours, longer if you launch closer to Sechelt.

Tuwanek to Kunechin Point, about 4 or 5 hours.

Tuwanek to Nine Mile Point, west to Halfway Beach, south to Piper Point and back to Tuwanek, 4 to 6 hours, depending on the route and your skill level.

Narrows Inlet and Tzoonie Narrows. Launch at Tuwanek, pass Nine

Mile Point, across Salmon Inlet, stopover in Storm Bay and up to Tzoonie Narrows in Narrows Inlet, 7 or 8 hours. It is also a good weekend trip, giving you lots of time to explore.

SNORKELLING AND SCUBA DIVING IN THE SECHELT AREA

Tuwanek Point Beach Dive

Fish do have personalities. Because they see so many divers here, they aren't easily frightened and you may have the unique experience of being stared down by a pan-sized fish. Around the island you may have the feeling of swimming in an aquarium, surrounded and followed by a colourful variety of decorative denizens. The bottom is like a garden planted with hydroids. Nudibranchs abound.

Access: From the main traffic light in Sechelt, turn east (inland) onto Wharf Road. Turn right on Porpoise Bay Road, which shortly becomes Sechelt Inlet Road for 9.6 km (5.7 mi). Keep left at the "Y" junction and follow the road to the water. A wooden archway marks the access to the gravel spit and dive. There are no facilities and limited parking. If you are planning a group dive, take as few vehicles as possible and, since there are no toilet facilities, make other arrangements. This does not mean going behind a bush, since there are no secluded spots.

Description: Primary, including snorkellers. Most divers swim out to the nearest island before heading bottomward and circling the island counterclockwise. If you plan a second dive, try the sheltered bay to the right of

*A diver and
a denizen exchange tips.*

your entry point. If you do so, the scenery is less spectacular but the fish are bigger and the seascape more varied.

Depth: Around the island, the bottom at its deepest is 21 m (70 ft), but the banks and walls are interesting all the way down. The sheltered bay is around 10 m (33 ft).

Hazards: Boats and fishermen. Tuwanek began as cottage country but now there are large numbers of permanent residents. In summer especially, the water abounds with boaters, many of whom are kids. There's lots of monofilament line caught on the rocks and some annoying abandoned anchor ropes to threaten you. Carry a good knife.

Artificial Reef *Chaudiere*

The Artificial Reef Society of BC placed this 109-m (360-ft) retired destroyer in Sechelt Inlet as one of several projects that will enhance the underwater environment by creating a habitat for a wide variety of species. This is one of the largest wrecks you may ever dive. The *Chaudiere* can be explored by most recreational scuba divers, but only those with specific training will reach the maximum depth or penetrate the wreck. But you will have lots to see even if you stay outside the ship and in relatively shallow water.

Sea growth abounds along most of the Sunshine Coast.

Access: 49°37.76'N 123°18.77'W. Chaudiere Bay is to the west of Kunechin Point. It is 8.9 nautical miles from the government dock in Sechelt and 9.5 nautical miles from the government dock in Egmont.

Description: Intermediate/ advanced. Mooring cans are provided. In addition there are 3 yellow cautionary buoys with ground tackle attached to the ship. These serve as ascent and descent lines. The planning done prior to sinking has increased the safety factor for those penetrating the wreck.

Depth: 20–39 m (66–129 ft)

Hazards: Travel from Sechelt involves crossing Salmon Inlet. Be aware of outflow winds. Travel from Egmont involves transiting Skookumchuck Narrows. Be aware of tide and current predictions.

Failure to use a descent line could cause you to miss the ship and land in the deep water alongside.

Failure to get back to a fixed line will lead to a free water ascent. Be aware of local boat traffic serving other divers.

WHERE TO STAY IN & AROUND SECHELT

Bella Beach Inn. Davis Bay. Phone: 885-7191. All rooms with ocean view, across from beach, Superchannel & TSN, restaurant. No pets. Accepts major credit cards.

Blue Sky Motel. 4726 Sunshine Coast Highway (101), Sechelt. Phone/Fax: 885-9987, toll-free 1-800-663-5177. Across highway from beach, sleeping and full kitchen units, cable TV, complimentary coffee. No pets. Accepts MasterCard, Visa.

Casa del Sol. 6564 Gale Avenue, N. Sechelt, V0N 3A0. Phone: 885-0900, toll-free: 1-877 399-2929. Fax: 740-8353. Waterfront home with ocean view, spa, golf discounts, non-smoking, no pets. Accepts Visa, MC.

Cozy Court Motel. Phone: 885-7723. Fax: 885-5969. 5522 Inlet Avenue. Mailing address: Box 1534, Sechelt, V0N 3A0. Combination baths, DD phones, cable TV, movie channel, ice machine, walking distance to beach, restaurants. Small pets accepted.

Davis Bay Bed and Breakfast. 4632 Sunshine Coast Highway (101), Sechelt, V0N 3A0. Phone: 885-5404. Fax: 885-7977. Waterfront home, ocean view, near beach, children welcome, no pets. Accepts Visa, MC.

Davis Brook Retreat Bed and Breakfast. 7079 Sechelt Inlet Road, Sechelt, V0N 3A4. Phone: 885-9866, toll-free:1-866-462-2922. Wooded country acreage, swimming pool, sauna, non-smoking, no pets. Accepts Visa, MC.

Driftwood Inn Hotel. Trail and Teredo (5454 Trail). Mailing address: Box 829, Sechelt, V0N 3A0. Phone: 885-5811, Fax: 885-5836. Waterfront, combination baths, DD phones, cable and movie TV, restaurant. Accepts major credit cards. Pets extra.

Eagle View Bed and Breakfast. 4839 Eagleview Road, Sechelt, Phone: 885-7225, Fax: 885-7208. Two bedrooms and two full guest baths in modern view home. Sitting room with TV, sundecks and garden access. Close to beach, swimming, store and dining. Full breakfast served. German spoken. No smoking or pets.

Four Winds Beach House and Spa. 5482 Hill Road, Blacks Site, C33, RR 2, Sechelt V0N 3A0. Phone: 885-3144, toll-free: 1-800-543-2989. Fax: 885-3182. Bedrooms overlooking the sea. Summer moorage in Cairns Bay. Massage therapist on site. No pets. Children welcome by special request.

Inlet View Guest House. 6937 Porpoise Drive, Sandy Hook, PO Box 1837, Sechelt. Phone: 885-4490, Fax: 885-8938 Self-contained two bedroom chalet sleeps eight. Queen-sized and double beds, futons. Ocean front solitude, access to hiking trail and boat dock for moorage. Kitchen, dining room, living area and hot tub.

Pacific Shores Bed and Breakfast. 5853 Sunshine Coast Highway, Sechelt, V0N 3A0. Phone/Fax: 885-8938. Spacious guest room with queen-

*The Wakefield Inn—a fine example of
a west coast building and a great place to enjoy the view.*

sized bed, fireplace, private en suite bath, carport and entrance. Located on secluded waterfront, with views of water and garden. Close to shops and restaurants. Full breakfast served, adult-oriented, no smoking or pets.

Porpoise Bay Provincial Park and Campground. A naturally wooded 61-hectare (152-acre) park 4 km (2.4 mi) out of Sechelt on East Porpoise Bay Road. Phone: 885-9019. Sandy beach, marked swimming area (no lifeguards), chum and coho salmon run in Angus Creek in season, access to kayak and canoe routes, special cyclists-only campsites, showers, flush toilets, group camping area (reservations for group camp required, phone 898-3678), sani-station, picnic area near beach. Cash only. Pets must be leashed.

Royal Reach Motel and Marina. 5758 Wharf Road. Mailing address: Box 2648, Sechelt, V0N 3A0. Phone: 885-7844. Fax: 885-5969. Waterfront units, kitchenettes available, combination baths, DD phones, cable TV, fridge, laundry, boat rentals, near pub, golf course and restaurant. Accepts major credit cards. Pets accepted.

Tranquility Bay Bed and Breakfast. 7651 Sechelt Inlet Road, Sechelt, V0N 3A4. Phone: 885-3442, toll-free: 1-800-665-2311. Fax: 885-9038. Waterfront home, hot tub, kayaking, diving and mountain biking available, non-smoking. Accepts Visa, MC.

Tucker's Inn Bed and Breakfast. 6966 Sunshine Coast Highway (101), Black Site, C11 RR2, Sechelt, V0N 3A0. Phone: 885-9077, toll-free: 1-877-266-9567. Custom built for B&B, view, hot tub, near beach, no pets. Accepts Visa, MC.

Wilson Creek Campground. 4314 Sunshine Coast Highway. Mailing address: Box 1653, Sechelt, V0N 3A0. Phone: 885-5937, Fax: 885-5445, toll-free:1-800-565-9222. 21 km (13 mi) north of Langdale Ferry Terminal, full hookups, washrooms, hot showers, laundry, sani-station, fire pits, seasonal outdoor pool, pull-through and creekside sites, arts and crafts store. Close to beach, fishing, golf, grocery, restaurant. Accepts MasterCard, Visa. Pets accepted.

DINING IN AND AROUND SECHELT

As prices change with the economy we have used $ signs to indicate relative prices.

$ means 2 people can eat, have a bottle of wine (if licensed) and get out for under $30 or so. $$ is $40–$50 and $$$ is over $50.

"Downtown"

Golden City, 5550 Wharf Road; 885-2511. Chinese and Canadian cuisine. Delivery. Closed Tuesday. Sunday smorgasbord. $$

Kafe Amigo, 4-5685 Cowrie; 740-0080. Lunch menu—soups, quiches, etc. Coffees. $

Old Boot Eatery, 108a-5530 Wharf Street; 885-2727. Italian cuisine. $$

Pebbles, foot of Trail Avenue on the Esplanade; 885-5811. Waterfront; breakfast, lunch and dinner, specializing in seafood. Reservations recommended. $$$

Village Restaurant, Cowrie Street at Inlet; 885-9811. Steaks, pasta, seafood. Breakfast, lunch and dinner. $$

Davis Bay

Beach Buoy Take Out & Restaurant, 4774 Sunshine Coast Highway; 885-3715. Fish & chips, burgers, chicken. $

The Wharf Ichiban Restaurant, 4748 Sunshine Coast Highway (101); 885-7285. Japanese Cuisine. $$$

Porpoise Bay

Blue Heron Inn, 5591 Delta; 885-3847, or 1-800-818-8977. West Coast cuisine in a seaside setting, waterfront patio. Reservations required. Wednesday to Sunday. $$$

Keepers, 5764 Wharf Street; on Porpoise Bay; 885-4994. Seafood. $$$

HALFMOON BAY

There is no major shopping district in Halfmoon Bay (pop. 1,656), but there is a truly general General Store that stocks everything you might need, and two seaside restaurants with impressive menus.

From the traffic light in Sechelt, drive 7.4 km (4.4 mi) north and turn left at the Redrooffs Road sign. Over its 10 km (6 mi) length, this meandering, uniquely named road which parallels the Sunshine Coast Highway offers just about every coastal landscape: from wildland to suburbia, sea level to mountain highway.

The road quickly takes you to Sargeant Bay Provincial Park with its fine sandy beach, picnic facilities and hiking and nature trails. A little farther on you will find Coopers Green regional park—a popular destination for scuba divers. Recreational boaters line up here to take advantage of the free boat launching ramp. Kids can have fun playing on the sandy-pebbly beach and exploring the tidepools. A small island offshore is easily accessible at low tide and provides more opportunities for exploration. Be aware of changing tides.

A popular resort was once located nearby—tourist cabins, all with red roofs. The owner came up with the archaic spelling for "Redrooffs Resort." You may still hear the area, as well as the road, called Redrooffs. The bay itself was once called Cod Bay. It is still a spot to fish for cod and salmon.

The Redrooffs Circle Trail, actually an easy walk of a few minutes,

Halfmoon Bay,
seen from the government wharf,

begins on Mintie Road at the small grassy park. This 1 km (.6 mi) trail is all that's left of the original Redrooffs Trail that at one time went all the way to Sechelt, and later to Coopers Green. The park is a great place for a family outing. A cosmopolitan mixture of domestic and wild fowl make their headquarters at the mouth of tiny Halfmoon Creek and in late fall, there is a salmon run in the creek.

"Downtown" Halfmoon Bay was the site of a post office for nearly a century but it was closed a few years ago as part of the government's move toward increased efficiency through decreased service. The Halfmoon Bay Store on Mintie Road is still the centre of things and you'll find nearly everything the happy camper needs to stay happy. Next to the store is the Upper Crust, a bakery, café, gourmet food and gift store. At the foot of Mintie is the government wharf, once a stop for the Union Steamships. There are some great views from here.

A black oystercatcher on the job at Cooper's Green.

Redrooffs rejoins the Sunshine Coast Highway shortly past Mintie Road, forcing the tourist to make another choice to turn left or right.

Turning right will take you to Trout Lake for good freshwater fishing and swimming, the head of the Trout Lake hiking and biking trail, Trout Lake Forest Service road and more trails, or access to the Caren Range and Canada's oldest forest.

On the other side of the highway from Trout Lake an extensive trail network leads to Sergeant Bay Provincial Park, Triangle Lake and Coopers Green regional park (for more information see pages 77-80). Side trails with names like Datsun Alley, School Daze and Pterodactyl were built with the help of local elementary school students and are popular with hikers and mountain bikers.

If you turn left from Redrooffs, take another left turn onto Mercer Road to find two fine restaurants and accommodation at the Jolly Roger and Lord Jim's.

Looping back onto the Highway from Mercer, you continue to Pender Harbour.

Merry Island Lighthouse

Merry Island, the small rocky island just south of Halfmoon Bay,

The Merry Island light station.
Plans are underway to automate most west coast light stations.

occupies a strategic position separating Welcome Pass and Malaspina Strait. In 1901, Vancouver ships' captains pointed out to the federal government that shipping was increasing, "owing to the advent of eastern Capital employed in the development of fisheries, logging and mineral resources of our northern coast." According to Donald Graham in his book *Lights of the Inside Passage*, "When the profits of eastern capitalists were at stake, Ottawa could move with breakneck speed. The light went into service within a year."

Will Franklin and his wife were the first lightkeepers and preempted the rest of the island as a farm. Franklin was issued a hand horn and a salary of $360 per year. (All lighthouse keepers were notoriously underpaid and were forbidden to leave their posts without written permission. They were allowed vacations only if they paid replacement staff out of their own pockets.) The old hand horn was replaced with diaphone horns in 1924, the same year a radio station was established at the island.

After retiring in 1932, the Franklins remained on their farm until 1954, when declining health prompted them to move to Vancouver. By that time, George Potts had taken over the stewardship of the Merry Island light, one of the most demanding of all the Inside Passage lights, but was not given an assistant. In a letter he complained: "I am on the go from daylight to 9 p.m. every day without a single break. I had one period this winter when I went 14 days without my clothes off and got only 10 hours sleep in that time."

Though the government is pursuing a long-range plan to destaff west coast light stations, Merry Island still had a lightkeeper in 1997.

The Country Fair of Halfmoon Bay

This popular fair is usually held the second weekend in July at Coopers Green Regional Park. As well as sports tournaments and arts and crafts, the fair also sponsors a road rally, pancake breakfast and community dinner. The Volunteer Fire Department is also on hand selling hamburgers, ice cream and cotton candy.

Parks in the Halfmoon Bay Area

Sargeant Bay Provincial Park: This park offers a long sandy beach with lots of logs for lounging against, lots of places to picnic, and lots of opportunity for nature study, including a fish ladder and beaver dam. (The two don't work very well in combination: the beaver insists on blocking the water flow in the fish ladder. Volunteers regularly clear the dams from the ladder. The beavers are equally determined.)

It was through the efforts of a group of dedicated citizens that the provincial government took over this property as parkland. Continuing efforts by the Sargeant Bay Society have resulted in other improvements.

There is no camping allowed here.

From the upper part of the park, you have access to Triangle Lake hiking trail and the Trout Lake hiking and mountain bike trail.

Access: Turn left onto Redrooffs Road from Sunshine Coast Highway 7.4 km (4.4 mi) north of Sechelt. Follow Redrooffs 1.7 km (1 mi) to the park.

Coopers Green Regional Park: At low tide, a small sandy spit is exposed at this waterfront park, but swimmers generally use beach shoes to protect themselves from the mostly gravel beach. Other amenities include a boat ramp, public washrooms, a barbecue pit, a refreshment stand open in the summer, a large grassy area, picnic tables and some of the best sunsets on the Sunshine Coast. A large rock just offshore is an ideal place for young explorers and a popular scuba diving spot.

Access: Coopers Green Regional Park is on Redrooffs Road, 8.7 km (5.2 mi) from its southern junction with the Sunshine Coast Highway. It is 1.6 km (1 mi) from the northern junction of Redrooffs Road and the highway.

See also *Smuggler Cove Provincial Park* below.

HUMMINGBIRDS

Two varieties of hummingbirds can be seen on the Sunshine Coast: the Anna and the Rufous. The Anna is the only hummer to remain on the West Coast over the winter. The iridescent green and rose tint on the throat and crown of the male is unique, as is the display flight which combines a long, steep dive with a loud popping sound at the bottom, ending halfway up—a "J" motion. The Sunshine Coast is the extreme northern end of the Anna's habitat.

The Rufous has a distinctive orange tinge and is more pugnacious than the Anna. Its common calls are a soft *tchup* and a squeal which sounds something like *zeee-chuppity-chup*. Its display flight is a complete circle.

Hummingbirds frequent spots where nectar can be gathered. Columbine and fireweed are favourites. They also gather in large numbers around the nectar feeders thoughtfully provided by many resort keepers and homeowners.

Hiking the Caren Range

The Caren Range forest has been described as the oldest in Canada. There is no record of logging or forest fires, so the surviving parts may date back to the last ice age. Some individual trees have an estimated age of nearly 2,000 years. One yellow cedar stump whose centre had rotted out still retained 1,827 annular rings. The lost part could easily have accounted for another 200 years.

The oldest mountain hemlocks in Canada are found here. And here Friends of the Caren found the first recorded nesting site of the marbled murrelet. The Caren range is also home to Barrow's goldeneye, Vaux swift, Swainson's thrush and the extremely rare Bay lynx, a large (German shepherd-sized) wildcat found only in the Caren and Tetrahedron ranges.

For access to the Caren Range, see the chapter on four-wheeling.

Smuggler Cove Provincial Park

According to Bill Wolferstan's cruising guide to the Sunshine Coast (see appendix), a smuggler named William "Pirate" Kelly used the cove as his headquarters as he smuggled Chinese labourers from Vancouver to the US a hundred years ago. The story has it that he kept the illegal emigrants bound with chains in case his smuggling vessel should be stopped by the American Coast Guard. If that happened, the "chain gang" would be forced to jump overboard, presumably to sink like stones. (This perilous journey to the States cost $100 in turn-of-the-century money!) The cove also became a refuge for American boaters during Prohibition, and according to Wolferstan, the thirsty sailors saluted the King of England with this little ditty:

Four and twenty Yankees feeling rather dry,
Sailed into Canada to have a drink of rye.
When the rye was open, they all began to sing,
"God bless America, but God save the King."

Today, Smuggler Cove is a popular marine park and boasts some of the most beautiful scenery on the Sunshine Coast. Unlike most marine parks, it can also be reached from land, giving walkers as well as boaters a view of the almost-hidden cove which is one of the most popular anchorages on the coast. In the summer, it's not unusual for 20 or 30 boats to be anchored here.

The hiker will enjoy beautiful views of Georgia Strait and Welcome Passage and the chance to explore the extensive rocky shoreline.

Access: This park can be accessed by boat at the north end of Welcome Passage, or by vehicle by turning off the Sunshine Coast Highway at Brooks Road (north of Redrooffs), 15.9 km (9.5 mi) north of Sechelt. Follow the Smuggler Cove Provincial Park signs for 5 km (3 mi) to the park. There is a parking lot at the entrance.

Hiking Time/Distance: 2 hours for the 3.4-km (2-mi) round trip. A variety of shorter walks are also possible. In 1996 the trails were upgraded and extended.

Description: Primary. Remarkably flat, wide trails. An interesting trail for nature lovers, it winds through some swampy areas that are full of magnificent groves of skunk cabbage in spring, and through some territory favoured by garish toadstools in the fall.

At the little cove you have the option of carrying on to the outer peninsula to enjoy shoreline vistas or taking the trail to the left past the outhouse to a rocky beach a few hundred yards away.

There are also 3 or 4 camping spots at the head of the cove; however, there is no fresh water available so intrepid campers must pack in their own.

You will notice three small cabins located on islands in Smuggler Cove. These were built before the provincial government created the park.

Triangle Lake Hiking Trail

This lake lies immediately below the trail viewing platform. Access to the lake is specifically discouraged as the marsh is a peat bog and very delicate ecologically.

Look for eagles, huge yellow arum (when skunk cabbages get as big as these, they deserve to be dignified by a more noble name!) and water lilies with leaves almost a yard in diameter.

Access: 7.4 km (4.4 mi) north of Sechelt, turn left on Redrooffs Road. Follow the signs to Sargeant Bay Provincial Park. Park on Redrooffs by the yellow gate where the trail begins, or turn left to the parking area.

Hiking Time: Allow 3 hours for the round trip.

Description: Intermediate. It's a steady climb. Because of the delicate ecology of the area, the Triangle Lake trail is designated for hikers only.

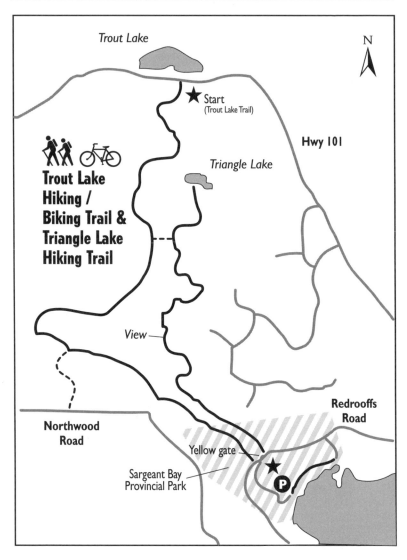

Trout Lake

N

Start
(Trout Lake Trail)

Hwy 101

Triangle Lake

**Trout Lake
Hiking /
Biking Trail &
Triangle Lake
Hiking Trail**

View

Redrooffs
Road

Northwood
Road

Yellow gate

Sargeant Bay
Provincial Park

P

However, there is a hiking/biking trail that follows a similar route and starts and/or ends up where you are beginning (see Trout Lake Hiking and Biking Trail).

The 3.6-km (2.2-mi) trail meanders through an alder grove, climbs along the creek and then passes through second growth cedar. About halfway up the trail, there is a lookout 100 m (110 yd) off the main trail. Early in the year, the wildflowers are in bloom, but by July, only a few foam flowers and the tiny blue self-heal remain. However, you can impress visitors if you know the Latin name for self-heal— *Prunella Vulgaris*.

One of the most interesting spots is a rock ledge covered with a lichen found nowhere else along the route and, alongside the ledge, a stand of arbutus. This is a good spot for a rest before tackling the last leg of the trail. About 600 m (.4 mi) before the lake, the trail divides: to the left, a 2.4-km (1.4 mi) walk to Trout Lake, and to the right, the last portion of the trail to Triangle Lake.

Trout Lake Hiking and Biking Trail

Trout Lake stands at an elevation of approximately 500 m (1,650 ft). The trail meanders through a wide variety of ecosystems all the way down to sea level, joining the Triangle Lake Trail at about the 2.4-km (1.4 mi) mark. This hike offers magnificent views, in season, of skunk cabbage, reeds, Douglas squirrels, and birds, birds, birds. Toward the bottom, it goes through an area that was clearcut and then reforested, now an example of how a forest regrows.

The hike may sound daunting because of the large change in elevation, but if you plan the hike using two cars, the trip becomes mostly downhill.

For bikers, this moderate to difficult route is also known as "Little Knives." It is called this for a reason. When the trail was cleared, many saplings were cut off about 15 cm (6") from the ground, and on an angle. If you wipe out on this one you stand a chance of being skewered. The best advice is: Don't wipe out.

Trout Lake. Yes there are trout—also, in season, swimmers and skaters.

Access 1: Take the Sunshine Coast Highway to the south end of Trout Lake and park. The beginning of the trail is just across the highway from the Trout Lake sign. The trailhead is marked, but is sometimes difficult to spot amongst the undergrowth.

Access 2: Turn left onto Redrooffs Road from the Sunshine Coast Highway 7.4 km (4.4 mi) north of Sechelt. Follow Redrooffs to Sargeant Bay Provincial Park. Park on Redrooffs by the yellow gate across the road from the beach where the trail begins, or turn into the beach parking area.

Hiking Time/Distance: 6 km (3.6 mi) and 2 hours each way (hiking), but read on.

Description: Beginner to Intermediate. When planning this hike, consider the two-car luxury route. This is one of the best hiking deals around. In a country where everything seems to be uphill from where you start out, or where a downhill start commits you to an uphill return, it's a treat to be able to coast. Park one vehicle at the Sargeant Bay end, then drive up to Trout Lake in the other. Note: Don't forget to go back for the other car.

BIKING IN THE HALFMOON BAY AREA

Trout Lake Bike Loop

This bike loop provides lots of good views over the water and easy access to other trails.

Access: Sunshine Coast Highway, 10 km (6 mi) north of Sechelt to Trout Lake. Park anywhere off the highway.

Time/Distance: 1.5 hours, 15 km (9 mi).

Description: Intermediate. Trails are marked clockwise with the biking symbol or a double band of yellow paint. From Trout Lake, head north up the highway and turn right on Trout Lake Road at 200 m (220 yd). Follow the logging road for 2.2 km (1.3 mi) to the Halfmoon Bay Forest Service Road. Turn right. The road forks after 1.6 km (1 mi). Take the right fork for 2 km (1.2 mi) where you will leave the main road. Take the right hand branch and stay on it for 7 km (4.2 mi). Carry on through the overgrowth, past a small pond and under the powerlines to finish up at the highway. Turn right and head back to Trout Lake.

Note: The lake is the water supply for those who live nearby. Please do not pollute it.

Carlson Lake Bike Loop

This bike route offers great views of Carlson Lake and Sechelt Inlet. (See map on page 82.)

Access: Follow the Sunshine Coast Highway 12.3 km (7.4 mi) north from Sechelt to Trout Lake Road (which leads to the Halfmoon Bay Forest Service Road). Take the main branch for either 6 or 12 km (3.6 or 7.2 mi). You can begin at either location as the route follows the main branch for this stretch. It is your choice whether you begin or finish with the long (6-km/3.6-mi) granny-gear climb.

Time/Distance: 2.5 hours, 21 km (12.6 mi).

Description: Intermediate to Advanced. The markers (a mountain bike symbol or a double band of fluorescent orange paint) are placed for a clockwise circuit. Most of the route is on old logging roads in poor condition and overgrown with fir and alder.

From the first starting point noted above (6 km/3.6 mi up the main branch of the forest road), continue for another 6 km (3.6 mi) to the intersection (the 12 km/7.2 mi point). Turn right, carry on for 2 km (1.2 mi) through the overgrown area and turn right again. You should now be under the powerlines. After another 600 m (660 yd) which includes a 100-m (110-yd) descent, follow the skid trail for 200 m (220 yd) and turn left on the

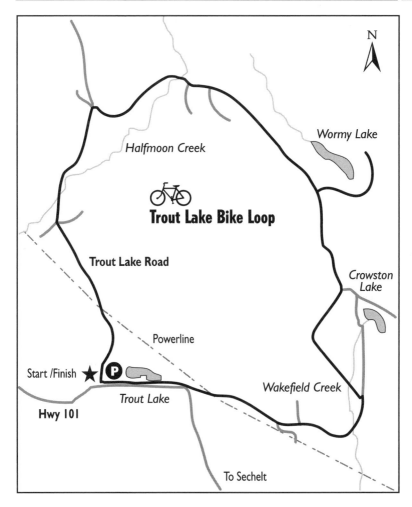

logging road. Stay on what looks like the main road. Intersections that could be confusing are marked. About 7 km (4.2 mi) from the powerlines you will pass a lake on the left and come to a bridge that is in poor condition. Cross it. Depending on which point you started the ride, you will arrive back at your vehicle after either 2.5 km (1.5 mi) or 8.5 km (5.1 mi).

Lyon Lake Bike Loop

The loop takes you through some of the oldest forest in Canada and offers magnificent views of the Strait of Georgia, Vancouver and Texada Islands, Jervis Inlet, Narrows Inlet, Salmon Inlet and the Coast Mountains. (See map on page 83.)

Access: Follow the Sunshine Coast Highway north from Sechelt for 12.3 km (7.4 mi). Turn right at Trout Lake Road (which leads to the Halfmoon

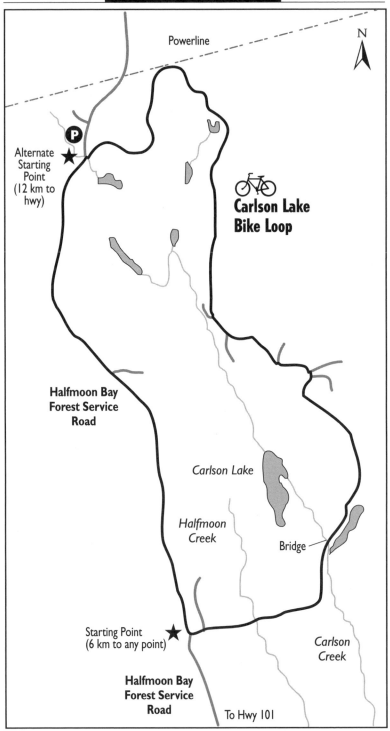

N

Powerline

Carlson Lake
Bike Loop

Alternate
Starting
Point
(12 km to
hwy)

**Halfmoon Bay
Forest Service
Road**

Carlson Lake

*Halfmoon
Creek*

Bridge

Starting Point
(6 km to any point)

*Carlson
Creek*

**Halfmoon Bay
Forest Service
Road**

To Hwy 101

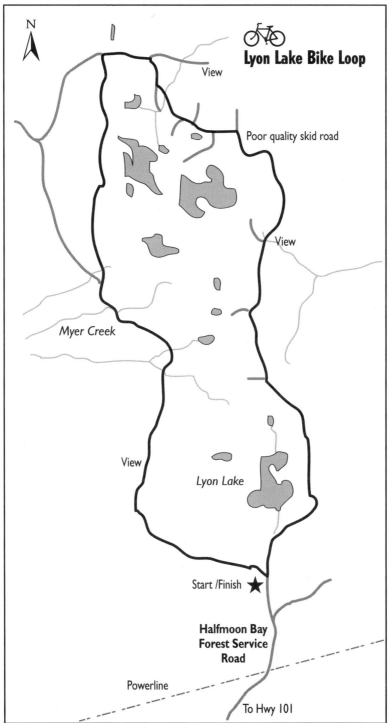

N

🚲
Lyon Lake Bike Loop

View

Poor quality skid road

View

Myer Creek

View

Lyon Lake

Start /Finish ★

Halfmoon Bay Forest Service Road

Powerline

To Hwy 101

Bay Forest Service Road). Continue up the main branch of the Forest Service road for 16 km (10 mi). Take the left fork once you have passed the power-lines and carry on to the next fork. Start biking here.

Time/Distance: 2.5 hours, 17 km (10.2 mi).

Description: Most difficult. It is recommended you take this one clockwise. Follow the markers (a mountain biking symbol or a double band of yellow paint). At about 5.1 km (3 mi) you get your first treat: views of Pender Harbour and Sakinaw Lake. About here the road becomes steep and gravelly. Keep right as the road forks along the Caren main logging road for 1.5 km (1 mi) and again take the right fork. And right again in another 2 km (1.2 mi). The route becomes confusing at this point but has been marked. After another 2 km (1.2 mi) you will come upon an old skid road. Take this for about 200 m (220 yd) and left down the extremely technical, steep, rough, overgrown trail for about 500 m (550 yd). Follow the logging road right. It gradually improves over the final 6 km (3.6 mi).

Homesite Creek Bike Loop

This route offers great downhill and powerline riding.

Access: Follow the Sunshine Coast Highway north from Sechelt for 18 km (10.8 mi). Turn right at Homesite Creek Forest Service Road and park. The road is not obvious when you are heading north. It's just a bit past Homesite Creek, which is marked with a sign on the highway. A better indicator is an orange "trucks turning" sign.

Time/Distance: 1 hour, 8 km (4.8 mi).

Description: Intermediate to Advanced. Ride the loop counterclock-wise. The trails are marked with the mountain bike symbol or a double band of blue paint. Take the Forest Service road 200 m (220 yd) past the power-lines and turn left. The trail climbs for 3.5 km (2 mi) on an eroded, overgrown logging road. Turn left at the cutblock onto a much better logging road. Follow this for 100 m (110 yd) and turn left again. Follow this road for 700 m (.4 mi) along the powerline and left onto the old logging road. (If you come back to the powerline, you have gone too far.) This 5-km (3-mi) downhill ends at the highway, 1.3 km (.8 mi) west of the Forest Service road. Finish the loop on the highway.

SNORKELLING & SCUBA DIVING IN THE HALFMOON BAY AREA

Shore Dive at Coopers Green

This site offers an excellent shallow beach access. There is a variety of sea life to enjoy, including anemone, encrusting sponge, and hydroids. A very short swim will get you to the east side of the island. Dive the east half of the island only. On the west side, there is a traffic lane for small boat access to the launching ramp.

Access: Coopers Green Regional Park is on Redrooffs Road, 8.7 km (5.2 mi) from its southern junction with the Sunshine Coast Highway. It is 1.6 km (1 mi) from the northern junction of Redrooffs Road and the highway.

Description: Beginner to Intermediate. This is a very popular dive site because, aside from its underwater attractions, it offers sufficient parking and good public facilities. Be respectful of others as this is a multi-use facility. There is a good deal of small boat traffic here as well.

Depth: To 18 m (60 ft). Below this, underwater life thins out quickly.

Hazards: Be very careful to watch for small boats. Descend and surface along the side of the rocks. Storms and groundswell pound in here from the south. Visibility may deteriorate if either of these conditions exists. Log booms are frequently on the move or moored nearby.

WHERE TO STAY IN THE HALFMOON BAY AREA

The Adventure Hut, 7751 Redrooffs Road, RR1, Eureka Site, C-83, Halfmoon Bay, V0N 3A0. Phone: 885-4888, toll-free: 1-877-322-4888. Fax:

885-4889. Mountain-bike oriented hostel-style accommodation. Near beach, bike trails. Bike shop/rentals attached. Children welcome; pets by arrangement. Accepts Visa.

Burchill's Bed and Breakfast. 5402 Donley Drive (Middlepoint). Phone: 883-2400. Self-contained one-bedroom cottage can sleep eight. Saltwater, seasonally heated pool, kitchen with microwave, laundry, showers, no pets. Access to beach, rowboats, barbecue.

English Rose Bed and Breakfast. 9127 Redrooffs Road. Phone: 885-4748. Self-contained suite, oceanview, large garden, hot tub, swimming pool, barbeque.

Jolly Roger Inn. 10163 Mercer Road (off Sunshine Coast Highway north of Redrooffs). Mailing address: RR 2, Jolly Roger Site, C 7, Halfmoon Bay, V0N 1Y0. Phone: 885-7860. Waterfront 1 and 2 bedroom self-contained units with TV and washers/dryers. Pub, restaurant, marina, moorage, fishing, diving and kayak charters available. Golf packages. Convention facilities.

Lord Jim's Resort. 5356 Ole's Cove (off Sunshine Coast Highway north of Redrooffs). Mailing address: RR2, Ole's Cove Site, Comp 1, Halfmoon Bay, V0N 1Y0. Phone: 885-7038, toll-free 1-877-296-4593. Fax: 885-7036. Located on 9 waterfront acres. Cabins, deluxe rooms and suites, seasonal pool, games room, sauna. Restaurant, salmon fishing charters. Convention facilities.

Priestland Cove Bed and Breakfast. 5625 O'Brian Road, Halfmoon Bay. Phone: 885-3764. Self-contained two-bedroom cottage with patio and kitchen. Ocean view, no pets.

Seawind Bed and Breakfast. 9207 Regal Road, Halfmoon Bay. Phone: 885-4282, toll-free: 1-888-999-5993. Private entrance, queen-sized beds with en suite shower, ocean view. Games, library and TV in guests' sitting room. Multi-course breakfast. Reservations recommended, no pets, smoking outside only.

DINING OUT IN HALFMOON BAY

$ means 2 people can eat, have a bottle of wine (if licensed) and get out for under $30 or so. $$ is $40–$50 and $$$ is over $50.

Jolly Roger Inn, 10163 Mercer Road (off Sunshine Coast Highway north of Redrooffs), 885-7860. Panoramic view of Secret Cove. Banquet facilities. Restaurant open seven days/week during summer, Thursday to Sunday during winter. $$$

Lord Jim's, 5356 Ole's Cove (off Sunshine Coast Highway north of Redrooffs), 885-7038. Waterfront restaurant with ocean view, continental cuisine. Reservations recommended. Limited hours during winter. $$$

Pender Harbour And Area

Throughout this book, we are guiding you through an area of almost constantly breathtaking scenery—each community, each area has its own charms, attractions, viewpoints and activities. There is a danger that we will run out of superlatives too soon, which would be a shame because in Pender Harbour there are two viewpoints that will literally render you speechless. (Each requires a substantial hike, so you'll be out of breath for more than one reason!)

Both viewpoints, Pender Hill and Mount Daniel, are nearly vertical climbs. Pender Hill is a bit shorter, but both are well worth the effort.

Each one gives you a panoramic vision of what the Sunshine Coast is all about—small communities clustered around beautiful inlets and islets, in a complex coastline that for many years challenged even the best road-builders.

You will see why spots that are separated by mere centimetres on the

Pender Harbour from the air.
You can see why boats were the only practical way to get around for many years.

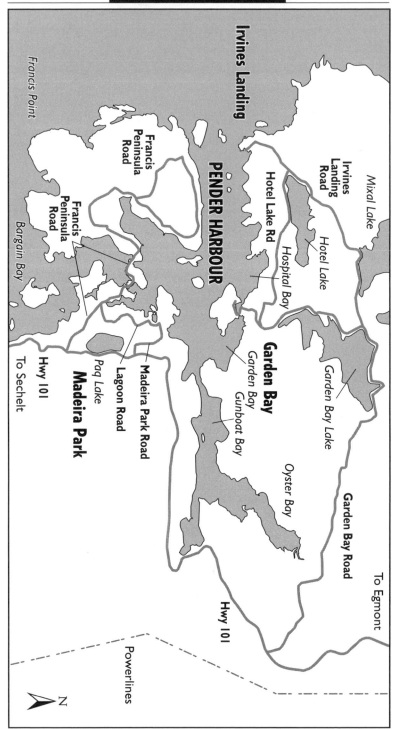

*A fine old wooden boat
dreams of better days.*

map are half an hour apart by car; why even the birds and bees have given up phrases like "as the crow flies" and "beeline" when giving directions. You will see why boats were the only practical way to get around for many years, and still make a lot of sense. Luckily, rentals are widely available and there are limitless destinations.

As we were going to press with this edition of *Sunshine and Salt Air<*, a spectacular new provincial park was announced for Pender Harbour. The 200-acre Francis Point Provincial Park boasts over 3 km of waterfront fronting the Strait of Georgia. It is a day-use-only park which offers swimming, hiking, picnicking, and scuba diving. At press-time, there were no signs in place and primary access was from the end of Merrill Road, just moments from the highway. A five minute walk takes the visitor to Middle Bay where the hiker can continue on to the left or right. This park has remained virtually untouched by man for almost 100 years and is representative of one of the most endangered ecosystems in BC (dry coastal Douglas-fir). Visitiors are asked to keep off the moss, stick to paths, and not to light fires.

One of the first Europeans to visit the area, Captian George Vancouver, anchored here in 1792. He wasn't very impressed, describing the harbour as "a dreary uncomfortable cove..."

A hundred years later, The *Vancouver News Advertiser* described the harbour as "this beautiful water which has the distinction of being the first

*The Sundowner Inn, formerly St. Mary's Hospital,
hosts the return of the Mission boats every two years.*

land-locked harbour on the mainland north of Vancouver deep enough for ocean vessels." Not long afterwards this community, where all commuting was still done by water, was touted by the Union Steamship Company as a "West Coast Venice."

Irvines Landing—named for Charlie Irvine, who arrived there about 1880—boasted a hotel, saloon, post office and general store. By the 1920s, the Union Steamships called regularly at the Landing, and a dogfish oilery and herring kippery were operating.

There were still no roads in the area at the time. "Local travel was strictly a matter of taking a boat as far as you could and walking the rest of the way," said Al Lloyd in *The Peninsula Voice*. When the first school was established on Francis Peninsula, "children seasoned their p's and q's with a good dash of seamanship."

A major development in 1930 was the construction of St. Mary's Hospital at Garden Bay, now the Sundowner Inn.

During the 1930s, a road was pushed from Sechelt to Pender Harbour, built in part by men from the work camps at Wood Bay and Silver Sands. The road was paved in the 1950s, and the focus of the community changed from water transportation to cars. The steamship service, for so long the harbour's lifeline to Vancouver, was reduced and finally cancelled. Irvines Landing, the commercial hub of the community, lost its status to Madeira Park, across the harbour and right on the highway.

Today, Pender Harbour, with its many marinas, marine stores, hotels and repair facilities, is the major boating centre between Vancouver and Desolation Sound. The surrounding waters are among the most popular salmon sport fishing destinations on the coast.

The Sundowner Inn

The Sundowner Inn, at Hospital Bay in Pender Harbour, began its life as the lower Sunshine Coast's only hospital, built by the Columbia Coast Mission and the Pender Harbour community. Water travel was so important on the coast that it was another 11 years before a road was constructed from the hospital to nearby Irvines Landing Road.

When the hospital closed in 1964 it was renovated as a hotel and today is the centre for many activities. The former chapel, now a theatre, is the site of plays, readings and murder mystery evenings. The restaurant, once the delivery room, offers gourmet dining.

Every second year (the odd-numbered ones), the Sundowner Inn hosts the Mission Boat Reunion during one weekend in August. These magnificent old wooden boats, now lovingly restored, used to ply the coastal waters taking groceries, medical aid and the Gospel to isolated communities. Now they return, bringing their tales and memories for a weekend of history and entertainment.

SWIMMING NEAR PENDER HARBOUR

Bargain Harbour. Ocean beach access. From the Highway, turn onto Francis Peninsula Road. Take the first left, Bargain Harbour Road, and park at the end. Please respect the private property owners.

Dan Bosch Regional Park on Ruby Lake. Picnic facilities, and a great place to launch a canoe or kayak. Going north on the Sunshine Coast Highway, pass Ruby Lake Resort and watch for the sign about .6 km (.4 mi) farther on.

Francis Peninsula Road. Ocean beach access. Not much of a beach, and rocky, but a good spot for a dip. Follow Francis Peninsula Road from the highway across a small bridge. A few hundred yards beyond, the road runs briefly along the ocean. Park on the side of the road.

Francis Point Provincial Park. This is a new park so it may be some time before signs are erected. From the highway, follow Francis Peninsula Road for approx 3 km. Turn left onto Merrill Road and follow it to its end. Park and follow the path five minutes to the water. This is probably the best saltwater swimming spot in the area. Access and parking may change.

Garden Bay Marine Park. Ocean beach. From the highway, follow Garden Bay Road past Garden Bay Lake and turn left at Claydon Road. Look for the signs.

Garden Bay Lake. Always clean, warm water. Accessible from Garden Bay Road.

Katherine Lake Regional Park. Offers warm water on a small still lake. The sandy beach with its gentle drop-off makes it an ideal place for small children. Take Garden Bay Road 4 km (2.4 mi) from the Sunshine Coast

Highway. Watch for the sign on your right.

Martin Road. Ocean beach access. Follow Francis Peninsula Road from the Highway 6.5 km (3.9 mi) to Martin Road. Look for a trail leading down to the beach from the junction.

Sakinaw Lake. Small sandy beach. Follow the Highway past Garden Bay Road for about 9.5 km (5.7 mi) to Sakinaw Lake Road. Turn left and follow the road to its end.

HIKES IN THE PENDER HARBOUR AREA

Mount Daniel Hiking Trail

The payoff to this trail is all at the top. On the way up there is nothing but ferns and forest, but once you're there, it's amazing. From here, on a clear day, you can see why you never know what direction you are driving in Pender Harbour, with its complex inlets and islets. Directly below you can see Garden Bay Lake, Katherine Lake and Mixal Lake. Also at the top, you may see "moon rings," artifacts of a Native rite of passage. Legend has it that at puberty, girls were provided daily with food but otherwise isolated on the mountain. They assembled the circles of rocks to symbolize the moon. In the evening a girl would begin a ritual that might take all night—picking up each stone in turn and talking to it as if it were the moon. Other rock arrangements you will find are probably of more recent origin. The Happy Face almost certainly dates from the late twentieth century.

Access: Garden Bay Road is the first major intersection north of Madeira Park on the Sunshine Coast Highway. Look for the prominent Petro-Canada service station. Turn left off the highway and follow Garden Bay Road for 3.4 km (2 mi) to a wide opening and dirt road leading off to the left. In 1997, it was marked with a hand-carved sign. It is probably easiest to park just off Garden Bay Road; the short road to the start of the hike is rugged.

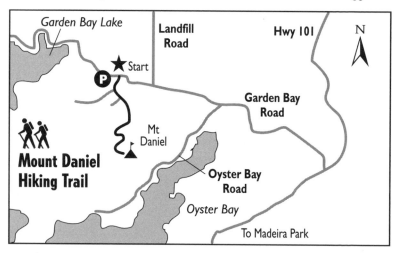

Hiking Time/Distance: 1 1/2 hours to the top, somewhat less on the descent. 3 to 4 km (1.8–2.4 mi) each way. Allow lots of sightseeing and recovery time at the top.

Description: Intermediate to Advanced. From Garden Bay Road, walk up the dirt road and take the first fork to the left. Continue up this road (ignore the short spur on the right) until the road peters out into a trail. From here on, the trail winds its way upward—unrelentingly upward. The return part provides its own form of torture as you always have the feeling of putting on the brakes.

Hazards: If you're goofy enough to stand too close to the edge you may also be unlucky enough to fall all the way to the bottom.

Mt. Daniel offers spectacular views and ancient "moon rings."

Pender Hill Hiking Trail

For the time it takes, this may be the most rewarding little jaunt of them all. In the days when Pender Harbour served as winter quarters for the entire Sechelt Indian nation and boasted a larger population than it does today, this was the lookout preferred by sentries on watch for parties of Yaculta or Haida war canoes, which might be expected to clear Cape Cockburn at any moment of any day. Although only half as high as nearby Mount Daniel, Pender Hill affords a clearer and more comprehensive view of the Pender Harbour area in its relation to surrounding waters and is much more quickly scaled. For the same reason, it is the best place for visitors to get an overview of the area's famous "drowned landscape" or for locals to climb free of their everyday lives and restore the broad perspective. You can sit for hours and watch trollers and plodding tugboats, luxury cruisers and streaking outboards come and go.

The entire area on top is open, gently benched and carpeted with areas of soft moss that can bring the somersaulting kid out of the tiredest old bones. The west slope supports what must be the nearest thing you'll ever see to an arbutus forest and the top is rich in the relatively rare "hairy manzanita," a type of miniature bush arbutus with bright red bark. You will also find it a good place to replenish your supply of wild herbs such as yarrow, juniper berry and kinnikinnick. In season wild violets, wild onions, tiger and chocolate lily (don't pick these two) give the area the appearance of a vast rock garden.

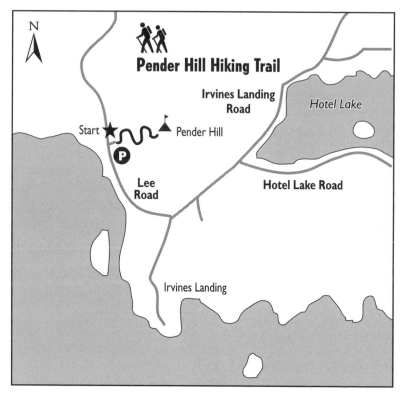

All in all, a perfect place for a picnic on a summer day with a cool ocean breeze or for an overnight campout under a full moon.

Access: From the Sunshine Coast Highway take Garden Bay Road, then Irvines Landing Road to Lee Road. Follow Lee Road for 1 km (.6 mi) and look for the Regional District sign.

Hiking Time/Distance: Half an hour up, a little less coming down.

Description: Intermediate. Short and steep.

Hazards: Loose rock and slippery moss.

CANOEING AND KAYAKING IN THE PENDER HARBOUR AREA

Pender Harbour has long served as a haven for cruising boats, both power and sail. It offers everything a boater could wish for, from fishing tackle to charts, fuel, grocery stores, laundry, ships chandlers, boat ramps and haul-out facilities.

However, not as well known are the incredible opportunities it offers as a canoe and kayaking destination. Whether a novice or expert, Pender Harbour's long, winding shoreline offers protected waters (for the most part) and is ideal for exploring. Not only is its maze-like saltwater shoreline a big draw, but four easily accessible lakes offer a host of freshwater paddling opportunities.

For those who don't have their own, kayaks, canoes (or motor boats) can be rented from many of the waterfront resorts such as Lowe's and Fisherman's Resort.

Hazards: Paddlers should be prepared for heavy pleasure-vessel traffic during the summer months. Although the waters of Pender Harbour and its lakes are relatively protected, it is always wise to check the weather forecast before you head out. This is even more important if you plan on circumnavigating Francis Peninsula, as you will be in open waters for part of the trip. Make sure to carry adequate safety equipment at all times

Paddling the Shoreline

Small cartop canoes or kayaks can be launched wherever a road runs alongside the shore (several are listed under "Swimming" on page 91). However, there are two official boat-launching ramps in the area. If you're in Madeira Park, the ramp is next to the public wharf "downtown". If you're on the Garden Bay side of the harbour, the ramp is at Irvines Landing. A small fee may be charged for launching. Rental boats can usually be launched directly from the rental location.

You don't really need a destination if you are paddling in Pender Harbour. We suggest you pack a picnic lunch, get a local chart and start

**Beautiful Sakinaw Lake,
one of the many jewel-like lakes in the Pender Harbour area.**

paddling. You're far more likely to run out of time before you run out of great spots to check out. If you keep an eye on your watch and where you've been and how long it took you to get there, you can spend from two hours to the entire day on the water.

The most obvious "trip" is to circumnavigate the harbour, starting at the Madeira Park public wharf. Alternately, you can leave from Irvines Landing (one of the stops along the route listed below). From the wharf at Madeira Park, head right (east) through the narrows into Gunboat Bay and Oyster Bay. Parts of these bays dry during low tide so keep a watchful eye underneath you. Oyster Bay, not surprisingly, is full of oysters, but they are part of a private lease and cannot be harvested due to a permanent shellfish contamination closure. After you've explored, paddle out the narrows and back into Pender Harbour. From here you can return to the wharf, or, keep to the right and carry on. Carrying on, you'll pass Garden Bay Marine Park where you can stretch your legs or enjoy your lunch. The Garden Bay pub sits at the head of the small bay just past the marine park and offers another lunch possibility. If you paddle back out of Garden Bay and west around Garden Peninsula, you'll find Hospital Bay, a wharf, store and the Sundowner

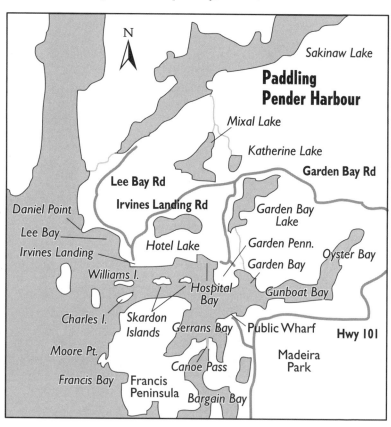

N

Sakinaw Lake

Paddling Pender Harbour

Mixal Lake

Katherine Lake

Garden Bay Rd

Lee Bay Rd

Irvines Landing Rd

Daniel Point

Garden Bay Lake

Lee Bay

Garden Penn.

Hotel Lake

Garden Bay

Oyster Bay

Irvines Landing

Williams I.

Hospital Bay

Gunboat Bay

Charles I.

Skardon Islands

Gerrans Bay

Public Wharf

Hwy 101

Moore Pt.

Madeira Park

Francis Bay

Canoe Pass

Francis Peninsula

Bargain Bay

Inn (see page 91). If you continue west, you'll paddle past the Skardon Islands in mid-channel and Irvines Landing (which has a restaurant, pub and boat launch) at the mouth of Pender Harbour. If it's not too windy, carry on west, along Lee Bay and to Daniel Point. The narrow peninsula at Daniel Point is a Regional District park and a wonderful spot to wonder around, eat lunch, or just relax and stretch your legs. From here, you can paddle back across Lee Bay and the mouth of the harbour, passing Williams and Charles islands. Hug the north shore of Francis Peninsula and you'll paddle into Gerrans Bay and back to the Madeira Park public wharf.

Another more adventurous voyage is to circumnavigate Francis Peninsula. Watch the weather before you undertake this one as it can get very rough on windy days. As with the previous route, you can start anywhere you like. The easiest may be to park alongside Francis Peninsula Road about 100 metres past the small bridge (over Canoe Pass/Bargain Narrows) that makes Francis Peninsula an island at half tides and better. There is a wide pullout here and you can carry your boat down over the rocks to the water. From here, you can either paddle back through Canoe Pass (or portage if there isn't enough water) and keep the Peninsula on your left, or head along the shore of Bargain Bay, keeping the Peninsula on your right. About halfway around the Peninsula, you'll come to Francis Bay, a perfect spot to pull out for lunch. This bay is part of the new Francis Point Provincial Park (day use only), though it may be some years before signs are erected. Please note that the shoreline around Moore Point is an ecological reserve and the boaters are asked not to land there. Carry on around the peninsula and you'll end up back at Canoe Pass and thence back to where you started.

The Pender Harbour Lakes

There are four lakes in the Pender Harbour area that make for some great paddling possibilities. Three of the lakes (Garden Bay, Hotel and Mixal) can be explored in a couple of hours, while the largest (Sakinaw) could easily be a full-day trip. Garden Bay, Hotel and Mixal lakes don't need any instruction. Simply park alongside the road and launch your boat. Be advised, though, these lakes provide drinking water to the community. Please respect them. Powerboats are not permitted. Sakinaw Lake is the largest lake on the Sunshine Coast. Powerboats are allowed. Boats may be launched from the end of Lee Bay road or the end of Sakinaw Lake Road.

DIVING IN THE PENDER HARBOUR AREA

Charles Island Boat Dive

This dive offers the opportunity to observe numerous wolf eel dens on the southeast point. Octopus are another common animal found here. Nudibranchs are plentiful in the shallow water.

Access: 49°44.76'N 124°02.64'W. Reaching Charles Island requires a very short boat trip to the mouth of Pender Harbour. Protected anchorage is available inside the rocks on the east side. The best dive site is in deep water on the southeast side. Anchoring is difficult here. Without a boat tender, plan for a long swim.

Description: Beginner/Intermediate/Advanced. Descend on the southeast corner of the island under the white sign. The most popular dive plan is to remain in this area or travel to the west. The shallow water to the east of this entry point lacks colour.

Depth: Life seems to thin out below 20 m (66 ft). However, there are wolf eel dens at 24 m (80 ft) at the entry point.

Hazards: Do not make any free water descents! It gets deep quickly as you go away from shore. The area has heavy boat traffic. Surface only

*Diver with gorgonian coral
near Pender Harbour.*

against the shore, and swim away from shore only when the pickup boat is present. The island is private property and "No Trespassing" signs are posted.

The southeast side frequently has onshore winds that can make boat handling and anchoring difficult.

Nelson Rock Boat Dive

Schools of rockfish live on the reef here, especially on the east side. The bull kelp forest just to the west of the light protects a collection of encrusting life on the shallow horizontal surfaces. The rocky features and formations of the reef make appealing designs and provide protected dens for octopus and wolf eels.

Access: 49°38.60'N 124°07.31'W. 2.4 nautical miles from the entrance to Pender Harbour. A flashing starboard-hand navigational aid is present on the rock.

Description: Beginner/Intermediate/Advanced. This rocky reef is in slightly open waters in Malaspina Strait. The reef is shallow and long but drops quickly on two sides.

Depth: 12-39 m (40-130 ft).

Hazards: This dive is in open waters exposed to wind and waves. Strong tidal flows can be expected. Be prepared. Make sure your boat is equipped with a good anchor.

Anderson Island Boat Dive

This dive offers spectacular examples of cloud sponge and marvellous rock formations.

Access: 49°30.74'N 124°07.7'W. 8 nautical miles from Pender Harbour across Malaspina Strait.

Description: Intermediate to Advanced and Technical. Plan to spend most or all of your time at the tip of the island, if possible. Cloud sponges can be found on the south point of the island, some as shallow as 21 m (70 ft). They live among beautiful rock formations. The deeper you go the larger they get. Technical divers receive further rewards as they explore the ranges below the limits of sport diving.

Depth: 20–39 m (66–130 ft) to technical.

Hazards: Anchoring is very difficult due to the depth of the water. Onshore breezes are common and build quickly. When a pickup boat is being used, travelling along the island can get you out of the worst of the weather. Make sure you clarify which side of the island you'll travel along. Travel across Malaspina Strait exposes you broadside to any developing sea conditions. Southeast swell in particular will be of short duration and quite steep.

Fearney Bluffs Boat Dive

This may be the area's best known dive site. It is excellent at all depths but is especially favoured for the lower ranges. Sponge and gorgonian coral are the main attractions here.

Access: 49°39.00'N 124°05.10'W. 1.5 nautical miles from the entrance light at Pender Harbour.

Description: Intermediate/Advanced/Technical. The south end of the prominent rock bluffs is the best area to dive. It has the most outstanding cloud sponges and, in the shallows, the area's largest concentration of encrusting life.

Depth: All ranges to technical.

Hazards: Anchoring is very difficult due to the depths and prevailing onshore breeze. Pickups can be difficult if a southeast breeze blows up. It's hard for a diver to swim away from the wall and the surface becomes choppy and broken. Your pickup system will need to be good.

Fishermen frequently troll along these bluffs and can be a significant hazard to divers. The best precaution here is an alert surface tender.

WHERE TO STAY IN PENDER HARBOUR

Madeira Park

Coho Marina Resort & Campground. "Downtown" Madeira Park. Mailing address: Box 160, Madeira Park, V0N 2H0. Phone: 883-2248. Shady sites, power and water, ice, showers, moorage, store, tackle, freezer, marine repairs. Pets accepted.

Lowe's Resort Motel and Campground. 12841 Lagoon Road, Madeira Park. Mailing address: Box 153, Madeira Park, V0N 2H0. Phone: 883-2456, toll-free: 1-877-883-2456. Fax: 883-2474. Housekeeping cottages, campsites. Cable TV, laundry, moorage, tackle rental and sales, freezer, salmon and cod fishing, covered and open boat rentals, kayaks, canoes, charters and guiding, beach and barbecues, divers' air. Accepts Visa and MasterCard. No pets.

Madeira Marina. 12930 Madeira Park Road, Madeira Park. Mailing address: Box 189, Madeira Park, V0N 2H0. Phone: 883-2266. Motel, RV park. Housekeeping units, full hookups, ice, washrooms, boat launch, marina, guest moorage, charts, saltwater licences, tackle, service, boat rentals and charters, marine repairs. No pets.

Silver Sands Resort, Madeira Park, off the highway just south of town. Phone: 883-2630. Beautiful sand beach, camping, trailer sites, cabins, boat rentals.

Garden Bay

Duncan Cove Resort. 4686 Sinclair Bay Road, Garden Bay. Mailing address: S15, C13, RR1, Garden Bay, V0N 1S0. Phone: 883-2424. Fax: 883-2414. Waterfront cottages, motel suites, campground, RV park. Showers, laundry, TV, boat rentals, moorage, ramp, tackle, bait, freezer. Pets accepted.

Fisherman's Resort and Marina. 4686 Sinclair Bay Road, Garden Bay; V0N 1S0. Phone: 883-2424. Fax: 883-2414. Waterfront cottages, RV park. TV, water hookups for RVs, laundry, showers, moorage, ramp, tackle, boat rentals, fishing charters, bait, freezer, near restaurants, store, post office. No pets in units.

Gunboat Bay Bed and Breakfast. 5202 Daniel Road, Garden Bay. Mailing address: S1, C17, Garden Bay, V0N 1S0. Phone: 883-9790. Three bedrooms, each with private bath and entrance. Full breakfast served, no smoking or pets. Ocean view, adult oriented.

Buildings appear to cling to the rocks along much of the Sunshine Coast's waterfront.

Irvines Landing Marina. Irvines Landing Road, Garden Bay area. Mailing address: RR1, S10, C9, Garden Bay, V0N 1S0. Phone: 883-2296. Housekeeping cottages and campground. Full hookups, water view, ice, hot showers, boat launch, moorage, marine pub, tackle, marine fuel, live bait, licences. Pets accepted.

Lakeside Motel and Campground. 4653 Hotel Lake Road, RR1, Garden Bay, V0N 1S0. Phone: 883-2354. Open mid-June to mid-September. Off-season phone: 941-2521. One-bedroom housekeeping units with fireplaces, lakefront campsites, showers, freezer, outdoor fireplaces, picnic tables, boat rentals, sandy swimming beach, trout fishing, volleyball, ping pong. Pets accepted.

Park Motel. 13483 Sunshine Coast Highway, Pender Harbour. Mailing address: Box 43, Madeira Park, V0N 2H0. Phone: 883-9040, toll-free reservations 1-800-665-4266. Fax: 883-9140. Kitchens, combination baths, cable TV, sports channel, sightseeing and fish charters arranged, near freshwater and saltwater fishing, hiking and golf course. Accepts Visa and MasterCard. Pets must be leashed.

Pender Harbour Auto Court. 4634 Garden Bay Road. Mailing address: Box 85, Garden Bay, V0N 1S0. Phone: 883-2244. Housekeeping cottages. TV, dining, grocery store, near boat rental, moorage and recreational facilities. Small pets.

Sundowner Inn. End of Garden Bay Road overlooking Hospital Bay. Mailing address: Box 113, Garden Bay, V0N 1S0. Phone: 883-9676. Fax: 883-

9886. "A lovingly restored historical landmark." Open April to September. All rooms overlook water, dining room, hot tub with a view.

DINING IN PENDER HARBOUR

As prices change with the economy we have used $ signs to indicate relative prices.

$ means 2 people can eat, have a bottle of wine (if licensed) and get out for under $30 or so. $$ is $40–$50 and $$$ is over $50.

Madeira Park

Frances' Hamburger Takeout, Madeira Park Road ("Downtown"), 883-9655. Famous for its burgers. Closed Sundays. $

Madeira Mercantile, Madeira Park Road, 883-2355. Deli-style takeout. 5:00 am to 5:00 pm daily. $

Pizza Pantry (takeout/delivery), Sunshine Coast Highway at Francis Penninsula Road, 883-2543. Pizza and submarine sandwiches. $

Seiners Cafe, 13823 Sunshine Coast Highway, 883-0023. Casual family-style dining. Open 7 days, breakfast, lunch and dinner. $

Garden Bay/Irvines Landing

Colonel Flounder's Drive-In, Hospital Bay, 883-2451. $

Garden Bay Pub & Restaurant, 883-9919 (restaurant), 883-2674 (pub). Overlooks the water. $$

Irvines Landing Marine Pub, 883-1145. Pub food overlooking the water. Cold beer and wine store. $$

Sundowner Inn, Hospital Bay, 883-9676. Overlooks the water. Seasonal. $$

EGMONT, EARLS COVE AND JERVIS INLET

Heading north on the Sunshine Coast Highway from the Pender Harbour area, it is about 18 km (11 mi) to the top end of the Sechelt Peninsula and the ferry terminal at Earls Cove. From here, a 45-minute ferry ride takes you across Jervis Inlet to Saltery Bay and to the upper Sunshine Coast.

Other than catching a ferry, the main attraction of this part of the coast is the small community of Egmont.

Q: What do the residents of Egmont call themselves?

A: Egmonsters, of course.

The calm water at Egmont
gives little indication of the rapids just around the corner.

The view over the north end of the lower Sunshine Coast.
Ruby Lake, left foreground, Agamemnon Channel, Nelson Island and Jervis Inlet

Egmont Road intersects with the Sunshine Coast Highway just a few minutes south of Earls Cove. Egmont is located 6 km (3.6 mi) from the highway. Along the way are some fine hiking, boating and camping opportunities.

Though the Forest Service campsite at Klein Lake has a reputation as a weekend retreat for yahoos, you might find yourself in sole possession, if your timing is right. There are several campsites around this secluded lake. We are told it is also the home of some fine fat trout. You may even be lucky enough to spot dinner plate-sized turtles sunning themselves. Please do not disturb. One of the really good hiking trails (Klein–Ruby Lake Trail) starts here.

A bit farther on is Skookumchuck Provincial Park and another spectacular hike to the Skookumchuck Rapids, the most impressive saltwater rapids on the coast. Hiking along a beautiful forest trail is its own reward. But both the Skookumchuck and Klein–Ruby Lake trails have other bonuses.

If you have two cars and a little foresight, the Klein–Ruby trail can be hiked entirely downhill, terminating near Ruby Lake Restaurant, while Skookumchuck Park is just a stone's throw from the picturesque Backeddy Pub and Restaurant in Egmont.

Nearby is Bathgate's Marina where boats can be rented. There are dozens of small coves and islands to explore—just be careful to keep away from the rapids.

Dive charters to the *Chaudiere* and other underwater destinations can also be arranged in Egmont.

Nelson and Hardy Islands

For those heading north from Earls Cove, the ferry travels around the northern tip of Nelson Island through the end of Agamemnon Channel, and Jervis Inlet to Saltery Bay. The sheer mountains and cascading waterfalls of this awe-inspiring inlet are renowned throughout the world, particularly the far reaches of Princess Louisa Inlet.

Someone once described Nelson Island, on your left, as "just a lot of rock and Christmas trees." But within those rocky bays and beneath those Christmas trees, some fascinating stories took place. From the time the first granite quarry opened in 1887, a succession of colourful characters scratched out a living on the island. They quarried, logged, fished, home-steaded or just got away from it all—most doing a little of each. Some came to escape World War I. Later, others tried a postwar soldier settlement. At

Harry Robert's log cabin on Nelson Island

Cape Cockburn in the thirties, the ingenious Harry Roberts (of Roberts Creek fame) built "Sunray," a sturdy log cabin with windows formed like the rays of the sun. It is one of the remaining monuments to island life during the Depression.

Granite from the Nelson Island quarry was used to build the BC Legislature in Victoria and the library at UBC. More quarries opened and closed; logging camps have come and gone; and recently strata title develop-ment and resorts are leaving their mark.

On your right in Hotham Sound, the late afternoon sun creates beautiful rainbows as it catches the spray from Freil Falls. The Harmony Islands are four charming islets about 800 m (1/2 mi) away. Jervis Inlet proper is approximately 1.6 km (1 mi) wide and 1,500–2,500 m (5,000–8,250 feet) straight up from high tide. For an unforgettable experience, charter a boat up the inlet, through the Malibu Rapids and into Princess Louisa Inlet.

Before the ferry makes a right into Saltery Bay, you'll see a long, low island on the left that seems to sprout out from Nelson's northern flank. This is Hardy Island, once a game sanctuary where Tom Brazil, another local character, swept the paths with a broom and put apples out on saucers for the deer. Master storyteller Judd Johnstone came to the island in 1930 to caretake its eastern half.

Today, only a handful of residents live on the islands year-round. Summer people swell the population for a few months before returning to their lives in the cities come Labour Day.

Almost all the place names in this area (Agamemnon Channel, Nelson Island, Hardy Island) honour Rear Admiral Sir Horatio Nelson, his second in command, Sir Thomas Hardy, or their officers, battles and ships. The "Telescope" in Telescope Pass and the "Blind" in Blind Bay refer to the fabled story of Nelson putting his telescope to his blind eye so he could ignore a command to retreat from the Battle of Copenhagen.

HIKES IN THE EGMONT AREA

Klein Lake–Ruby Lake Hiking/Biking Trail

The area around Klein Lake offers magnificent mountain vistas. You can spend a lot of happy hours around the lake, swimming, fishing and turtle-watching.

A bonus of this hike is the series of gnomes and trolls carved by Sunshine Coast artist Terry Chapman. They are visible from one of the cliffs during the hike.

Access: Option 1: Follow the Sunshine Coast Highway to Egmont Road and turn right. Turn right again at the North Lake Forest Service Road 1.7 km (1 mi) from the highway, and right again at the sign that indicates Klein Lake. This road is only moderately sedan-friendly; you may elect to park and walk at any time. This will increase your hiking time. At Klein Lake the road forks around the lake. Take the left-hand fork. The road gets rougher and parking spots harder to find the farther you go. Each time the road forks, take the right hand, downhill branch. The beginning of the trail is marked, but you may already have hiked 20 minutes before you get there.

Option 2: Park at Dan Bosch Park, located on Ruby Lake just off the Sunshine Coast Highway about 600 m (.4 mi) north of Ruby Lake Resort and several miles south of Egmont Road. The trail up to Klein Lake is across the highway. This option can be used as a two-car, lazy-boy hike. Leave one car at the park and drive up to Klein Lake in the other. You can hike both ways if you like, but remember you'll be climbing up about 500 m (1,650 feet).

Hiking Time: If you're on foot, about 1 hour each way. More if you hike up!

Description: Fairly easy if you start at Klein Lake; strenuous if you start at Ruby Lake or elect to hike the round trip.

Hazards: Children may need to be supervised along the part of the trail that hugs the cliff edge.

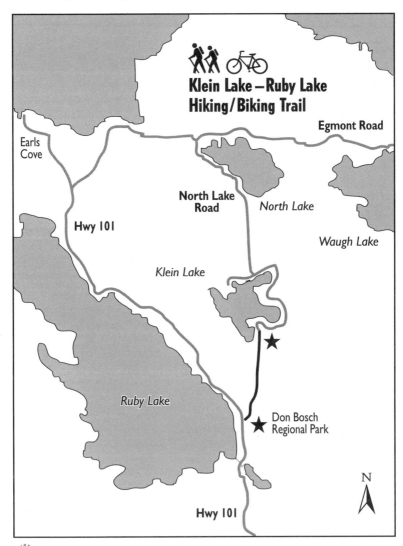

Klein Lake – Ruby Lake
Hiking/Biking Trail

Egmont Road

Earls Cove

North Lake Road

North Lake

Hwy 101

Waugh Lake

Klein Lake

Ruby Lake

Don Bosch Regional Park

Hwy 101

N

Skookumchuck Rapids

"Skookum" and "chuck" are Chinook words still in common usage on the West Coast. "Skookum" means strong or powerful, "chuck" means water. Skookumchuck is one of the West Coast's largest saltwater rapids, all the more amazing in that as the tide changes, it reverses. Best viewing times are posted at the beginning of the trail and are published in the local papers. Plan to be there an hour before and after a tide change, for, as spectacular as the rapids are at maximum flood or ebb, they flatten out to a dead calm and soon become just as spectacular in the other direction.

At low tide the bays reveal a colourful display of sea life: barnacles, urchins, sea anemones and mollusks. The action of the current causes the

The rapids at Skookumchuck—don't forget to take your camera.

creatures here to grow to extravagant sizes.

Access: Follow the Sunshine Coast Highway north to Egmont Road, about 20 minutes north of Madeira Park. Follow Egmont Road for 6 km (3.6 mi) and watch for the Skookumchuck Narrows Provincial Park parking lot on the right. Visitors are asked to hike, not drive, down the roadway that leads from the parking lot to the trailhead. Please respect the rights of private property owners by staying on the access road and keeping your pets leashed.

Hiking Time: 45 minutes to an hour to Roland Point, 4 km (2.5 mi) each way.

Description: Primary. The trail was built and is maintained by BC Parks and is wide and well cleared. There are information signs at the parking area and public toilets at both ends of the trail.

Hazards: Exercise extreme caution. There is little chance of saving anyone who falls into the rapids.

DIVING IN THE EGMONT AREA

Cosmic Corner Boat Dive

This dive provides the opportunity to experience a wide range of marine life including an abundance of encrusting life and big sponges and anemone.

Access: 3.7 nautical miles from the government dock in Egmont. The dive site is at Foley Head.

Description: Beginner/Intermediate/Advanced/Technical. There is one good shallow anchorage. You can dive right from that point. The shallow leg against the headland has a range of encrusting life, and after it drops off there are even larger and more varied sea creatures on the vertical walls. Those exploring the depths will find big sponges and anemone.

Depth: 12–39 m (40–130 ft).

Hazards: Crossing Jervis Inlet in a small boat may be difficult on a stormy day. You'll be broadsided with outflow winds.

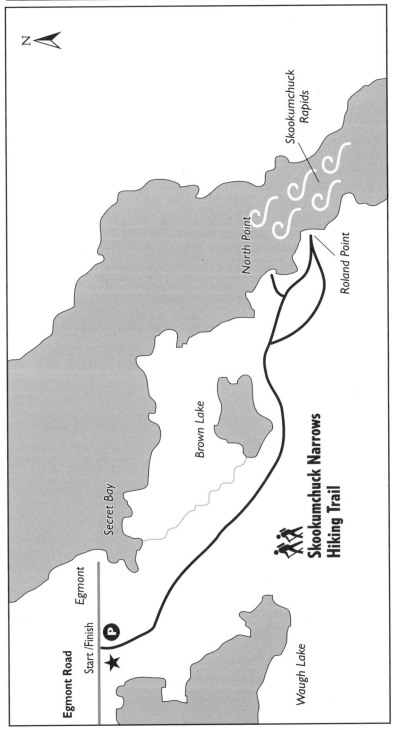

N

Skookumchuck Rapids

North Point

Roland Point

Brown Lake

Secret Bay

Skookumchuck Narrows Hiking Trail

Egmont

Egmont Road

Start /Finish

P

Waugh Lake

Bent Tree Boat Dive

This dive offers ample sea life to entertain all divers. At the deeper depths, cloud sponges and gorgonian coral can be seen. Technical divers who travel to the greatest depths, however, will swim among the largest, most spectacular specimens.

Access: 49°44.53'N 124°02.41'W. The northern powerline in the Agamemnon Channel is 7.5 nautical miles by boat from the entrance to Pender Harbour and 4.7 nautical miles from the government dock in Egmont. The dive site is below the marker on the east wall.

Description: All ranges to technical. Most divers think of this site as being advanced or technical.

Depth: Full range to technical.

Hazards: Due to the depths, anchoring is very difficult.

Park Wall (Skookumchuck Rapids) Boat Dive

This is one of the outstanding dives in the Pacific Northwest. There is a wide range of anemone life. Sponges and fish abound. Giant barnacles and other encrusting life dominate the more exposed points. Large predator fish hunt here.

Access: Along the wall below the North Point lookout at Skookumchuck Narrows Provincial Park.

Description: Intermediate/Advanced. The dive requires a great deal of planning due to the large amount of water flow created by the tidal exchange. Currents often exceed 10 knots and can reach 16 knots!

Bathgate's General Store is a landmark in Egmont.

Depth: 18–24 m (60–80 ft).

Hazards: Current! You'll need to dive on the slack. This generally means being on site and ready early. Slack water periods can be short (10–15 minutes) and build quickly. Coordinating a good dive plan with the surface tender is important. Nothing is more valuable than good local knowledge.

This is a main channel that will see a lot of boat traffic at slack tide, dive time. Be sure to stay against the wall when surfacing and descending. Current will be slowest against the rocks and on the bottom. Up-wellings and down-wellings in open water columns can move you quickly away from the dive site.

ACCOMMODATION NORTH OF PENDER HARBOUR

Egmont Marina Resort. Egmont. Phone: 883-2298. Waterfront cottages, campsites with power, washrooms, showers, laundry, store, boat launch and rentals, dive charters, kayak rentals and lessons, restaurant.

Ruby Lake Resort. Sunshine Coast Highway 10 minutes north of Pender Harbour. Phone: 883-2269. Lakeside motel, cottages. Wilderness walking trails, paddle, motorboat and canoe rentals, restaurant.

DINING NORTH OF PENDER HARBOUR

As prices change with the economy we have used $ signs to indicate relative prices.

$ means 2 people can eat, have a bottle of wine (if licensed) and get out for under $30 or so. $$ is $40–$50 and $$$ is over $50.

Ruby Lake Restaurant. Sunshine Coast Highway 10 minutes north of Pender Harbour. Phone: 883-2269. Italian fine dining, fresh seafood. $$$

Tom & Sherry's Place. Earls Cove ferry terminal. Phone: 883-9412. Cafeteria-style restaurant. $

Backeddy Marine Pub. Egmont Marina. Phone: 883-2298. Overlooks water. Pub and dining room. $

3

THE UPPER SUNSHINE COAST

SALTERY BAY TO POWELL RIVER

As the ferry from Earls Cove passes beneath the powerlines that stretch from the mainland to Nelson Island, on the right you'll see Elephant Point, which indeed looks like a fuzzy green elephant relaxing on its belly, its trunk pointing straight out into the waters of Jervis Inlet. You'll notice that the shore ahead of you mellows out into gentler slopes and smaller hills than those you've just left behind on the southern coast. The white tower standing high above the trees is the surge tank for the Stillwater power plant.

The ferry turns into Saltery Bay, where on your right you'll see the bustle of small craft, fish boats and sailboats at the government marina. From the creosote pilings a jealous seagull cries out at a friend waddling along the shore, a bright purple starfish dangling from its bill. A bald eagle dives for his dinner. Beyond the marina, a decrepit spillway is all that's left of a disused log-booming pond, where for years logs were dumped from trucks to tumble down the slope into the water. Nothing at all remains of the Japanese salmon saltery that operated here during the first two decades of the century. Jutting out from the shoreline on stilts, the saltery bought salmon from the Coquentet people of the Sechelt Band, who lived and fished in the area.

When you leave the terminal, you may want to stop at the Saltery Bay Mermaid Cove Provincial Park 1.8 km (1 mi) down the road. The little peninsula off the park campsite is alluring. Or the picnic site 2 km (1.2 mi) farther

**Saltery Bay Mermaid Cove Provincial Park
is a popular diving and camping site.**

up the highway, which offers a boat ramp as well as a good view of Hardy Island. After the turnoff to Stillwater at 10.9 km (6.5 mi) the highway goes over the huge penstock that takes water to the hydroelectric power plant at Stillwater. On the left is the towering surge tank that you saw from the ferry. Surge tanks don't actually store water, but rather even out the flow of water to the turbines.

Now and then from the highway you'll see sheep or cattle grazing contentedly, a reminder of how the early settlers spent years trying to tame the timber land into country farms. Pioneers like George Deighton, who came to

THE JOHNSTONES OF SALTERY BAY

Houses that can be glimpsed through the tall firs are part of the rich local legacy of Charlie Johnstone, who first visited this bay on his way up to Jervis Inlet in 1902. At that time it was not uncommon for men to row dugout canoes all the way to Alaska during the summer. They would catch fish for the canneries along the way, spend their nights in driftwood shelters on the shore, and return in the fall, trapping as they went. Charlie's son Judd (Forrest) Johnstone homesteaded in Jervis Inlet and on Nelson Island. In the mid-1950s, when the road was put through, six of Judd's children bought lots from Frank Jenkinson for $500 apiece, and moved over to Saltery Bay. Charlie would chuckle to know that almost a century after he first put in to shore, he has grandchildren and great-grandchildren still living there.

the Myrtle Point area around 1893–95, gave the magnificent trees away for 50 cents apiece or burned them, to get rid of the pesky things so he could raise sheep. None were more appreciative of his efforts than the local populations of cougars and wolves, which began felling sheep by the dozens.

Loubert Road heads down into Frolander Bay and Stillwater. Frolander opened a trading post in 1880 to buy furs from local trappers. In its early years Stillwater was called Scow Bay; there was no wharf so cargo scows came right up on the beach.

The landmark surge tank at Stillwater.

Sixty acres (24 hectares) on the west side of the Lois (Eagle) River is still a tiny reserve of the Coqueneets, known for their boatbuilding. They were friendly but shy when they traded baskets with the settlers for clothes or apples. In 1919, their population was devastated by the flu that swept through the area. Only buried middens and the fish traps they left among the rocks on the beach tell the story of these First Nations people.

If you are arriving for the Labour Day Weekend Folkfest, watch for the Lang Bay Road sign on your left. It leads down to scenic and sandy Palm Beach Regional Park.

Lang Bay was named for the Lang brothers —Tom, Harry and Fred—stepsons of Bob Simpkins, who settled in the area in 1911. In honour of their service in World War I, Wolfson Bay and Wolfson Creek, originally named for a German Consul, were renamed Lang.

In 1921 a freak southeasterly windstorm whipped along the coast,

THE MAN WHO DUG FOR FISH

In 1946 Frank Jenkinson retired from logging in Seymour Inlet and purchased an old Saltery Bay homestead. He watched raccoons scoop the "redd" or nest of salmon eggs from the gravel edge of a nearby creek bed, where the eggs and fry were stranded by falling water levels. Frank tried it himself, depositing the chum fingerlings in the main stream. News of this strange but environmentally friendly activity soon spread, and before long Frank found himself the star of a National Film Board short, "The Man Who Dug for Fish." For over a quarter of a century he dug fish, raising the numbers of fish returning to the stream from 600 to 25,000. In 1997, Frank reached his 100th birthday. You'll see his name on Jenkinson Road, the second road to the left as you drive off the ferry, although he left the area for Westview many years ago.

gusting to 160 kph (100 mph), downing colossal trees like pick-up sticks. Although fires were an annual hazard, in 1922 the worst of them burned south from Myrtle Point to Lang Bay, scorching a wide band along the foreshore. One of the survivors of the blaze was the school built in 1912, which is now the Lang Bay Hall, just past Lang Bay Road on your left (Dixon Road

This derelict bridge over Lang Creek
is a reminder of nature's powerful drive to reclaim the forest.

on your right). Another survivor was a small stand of trees known locally as the "Enchanted Forest." Evidently there are still 4 or 5 old-growth trees in this "forest," but it is unmarked and we can only say that it is somewhere in the area of Douglas Bay.

Just past Lang Creek, where the Powell River Salmon Society's spawning channel facility offers an inviting creek walk, is Brew Bay Road, a name that smacks of prohibition days and homemade hootch, although in fact it honours BC's first policeman. Zilinsky Road, originally the railbed for Elder Brothers Logging, is the next turnoff to the right. It will take you up to Nassichuk Road and the petting zoo and other attractions of Mountain Ash Farm.

Just past the Black Point area, the main shopping and video rental stop south of town, the countryside opens, allowing good views of the Strait of Georgia and Texada Island. If you wish to hike, cycle or drive through the backwoods hereabouts, watch for the Garnet Rock Trailer Park sign on your left in the Myrtle Point region (from the Saltery Bay ferry, 23 km/14 mi); the Duck Lake Road is opposite. This road is your access to a network of relatively flat hiking and cycling trails. If you follow it to the end you will come out at Haslam Road in the Cranberry area.

Past the Myrtle Point Golf Course, the highway drops down to pretty

THE PRAIRIE FARMERS OF KELLY CREEK

In 1924, 150 families from Saskatchewan, searching for a warmer climate, arrived on the steamer to view their new land on Zilinsky road. Purchased for $2.50 an acre, it proved to be poor farming soil for the ten or twelve families who, having seen the land, stayed to settle. Most were Rumanian and Ukrainian families of Greek Orthodox faith. These hard-working, independent people integrated into the larger community, but their origins can be seen in a tiny country cemetery across from the Mountain Ash Farm's Petting Zoo on Nassichuk Road.

STILLWATER: THE EAGLE RIVER AND NORTHERN RAILWAY

In 1906, John O'Brien began logging the area, and in 1908 he was joined by Dr. Dwight Brooks and M. Joseph Scanlon, who imported the name Stillwater from a town in their native Minnesota. The amalgamated outfit started The Eagle River and Northern Railway in 1909, and had it whistling 5 miles into the woods in its first year. In 1916 *The Western Lumberman* reported that they were cutting 5 million board feet per month, from Douglas fir stands that were reputed to be BC's finest. One 71-m (237-ft) giant was cut and dried to become a flagpole for Kew Gardens in London, England.

The railway ran for a total of 46 years. Brooks, Scanlon & O'Brien operated it until 1928, when the Robert McNair Shinglebolt Co. took it over. By 1955 truck logging was clearly the way to go, and Powell River's era of railroad logging came to a close. Along the highway today, it is common to see loaded trucks making their daily trips to the Stillwater booming grounds.

*The remains of
an old Sliammon fish weir.*

Myrtle Rocks Park, once the main camp of the Bloedel, Stuart & Welch logging company. Seagulls perch on the ragged pilings, the only remains of the 1911 railroad.

You're almost to Powell River, and suddenly at 29.3 km (17.6 mi) from the Saltery Bay ferry, a curve in the road brings you a panoramic view over Malaspina Strait. Aboriginal fish weirs (long rock-piled traps) on the beach below contrast with the distant stacks of the town's founding pulp and paper mill. A large cedar hangs over an azure sea crisscrossed by ferries and fishing boats. In contrast, an architect-designed modern home dominates the foreground.

Along this stretch of coastline, the orcas entertain from time to time and the urban eagles reign. There are two nests in the area: one just before the corner, on private property, and one on the side of the road almost opposite 3958 Marine (Hwy 101). It is not unusual to see two eagles perched in a tree at one time. Loons, herons, cormorants, scoters, mergansers, mallards, goldeneyes, harlequins, western grebes, ospreys, American widgeon and other migrating birds and ducks are familiar sights along this shore.

Watch for the Westview Viewpoint on the left, where you can park not only to enjoy the sights, but to appreciate a wall of history: hundreds of red brick tiles, each inscribed with the name of one of the area's residents, past and present.

FACES IN THE WOODS

This whole area has been logged for over a century. Watch the side of the road carefully; some of the old stumps have springboard-notch faces and wild huckleberry hair. Have the kids count them while you explain how the husky handloggers cut out the notches and inserted boards to stand on while they made the undercut on the straight part of the tree, then chopped and chopped, sometimes taking days to fall one tree. The stumps are high because the thick butt end took too long to cut through, and also tended to catch on trees and windfalls as the log was dragged through the forest by oxen.

WARNING: BEWARE OF LOGGING TRUCKS

Don't count on signs being posted on logging roads when they are being used by logging trucks! Always assume a loaded truck is just around the corner. If you should meet up with one, always yield the right of way. If you are planning to travel on a logging road to sightsee, access hikes, camp or take part in other recreation activities, call the Forest Service at 485-0700 before starting out.

SWIMMING SOUTH OF POWELL RIVER

Saltery Bay Provincial Park: Just north of the ferry terminal at Saltery Bay, on Highway 101. Ocean beach.

Eagle (Lois) River: Off Highway 101 below the Lois River Bridge, Lang Bay.

Palm Beach: Access off Highway 101 at Lang Bay.

HIKES SOUTH OF POWELL RIVER

The Sunshine Coast Trail

The completion of the Sunshine Coast Trail (SCT) in the year 2000 fulfilled a dream for the Powell River Parks and Wilderness Society (PRPAWS). Over 180 km (108 mi) long—more than twice the length of the West Coast Trail on Vancouver Island, it stretches from Sarah Point in Desolation Sound Marine Park, south to Saltery Bay (see map). Unlike the West Coast Trail, it is not a "do-or-die" adventure.

Since 1992, PRPAWS has dedicated itself to setting aside a protected corridor along the length of this unique trail and have gained the support of Weyerhaueser, owners of the surrounding forests. The hard-working PRPAWS not only developed the SCT but also undertake the maintenance.

The recommended trailhead is the cableline at Sarah Point. (Reserve your water taxi at Lund: 483-9749). Allow a day for every 10-15 km (6-9 mi) to be hiked. There are five sections, each with 2-7 shorter trails for a total of 30. It is fairly strenuous at times. You might like to try a 3-day hike to test your fitness before attempting the whole route.

Section I takes you into Hinder Lake water reservoir, then on to Wednesday Lake campsite. Most people find this enough hiking for the first day but some will want to continue through the stands of old growth in lovely Gwendolyn Hills down to more comfortable accommodation in Okeover Arm (see p 178).

Section II promises a variety of fantastic views—Gibralter and Gentle David, cascading waterfalls, pools, moss-hung rain forest, lakes, and more virgin timber. At last, the Scout Mountain loop leads to a pub/bistro on Powell Lake.

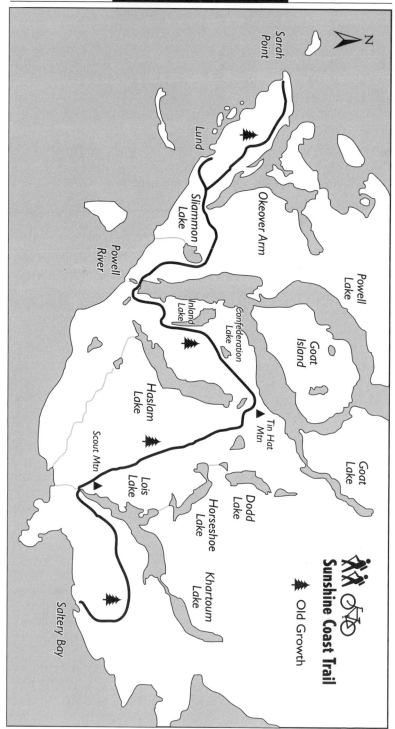

N

Sarah Point

Lund

Okeover Arm

Sliammon Lake

Powell River

Powell Lake

Inland Lake

Confederation Lake

Goat Island

Haslam Lake

Tin Hat Mtn

Goat Lake

Scout Mtn

Lois Lake

Dodd Lake

Horseshoe Lake

Khartoum Lake

Saltery Bay

Sunshine Coast Trail

Old Growth

Section III takes you from the Powell Lake bridge into Mowat Bay, across a sandy beach, part-way around the lake and up around the mountain into Haywire Bay campsite. From there you hike into Inland Lake where it's easy-walking and good fishing. The next link is more challenging, up a steep trail to Confederation Lake. There is snow on this high trail until late spring and there is only one cabin amid the spectacular views—first come, first served. Continue down to Fiddlehead Farm for comfort and sustenance.

Section IV treats you to a panoramic view of the ocean, islands and thirty lakes from atop Tin Hat Mountain. There are good swimming lakes on the descent through the virgin timber.

In Section V, travelling down from Goat Lake, you discover an old logging railbed, the Lois Lake Dam, then climb again to more breathtaking views on the Mount Troubridge summit before the final descent to Saltery Bay.

There are plans to provide huts or B&Bs at the end of each day's hiking as well as a sherpa service that will one day take hiker's large packs from one B&B to the next. For a virtual tour, visit www.sunshinecoast-trail.com. Guided tours may be arranged there or contact PRPAWS at PO Box 345, Powell River, BC, V8A 5C2. For a SCT Package, call PR Visitors Bureau at 1-877-817-8669 or Mail to: 4690 Marine Ave, Powell River, BC, V8A 1T9; Fax (604) 485-2822, Email prvb@prcn.org See also: www.roughlife.com

Lang Creek Hiking and Biking Trail

The first part of this trail is a demonstration forest. Signs identify trees and plant life. The hatchery on the other side of the creek holds every type of salmon except sockeye. Two million fingerlings of chum or chinook salmon can be seen in alternate years. For those with interest, workers at the hatchery are available to tell you more about the operation. (See map on page 122)

Access: Follow Highway 101 23 km (14 mi) north from Saltery Bay (or 9.5 km/5.7 mi south of the Westview ferry terminal in Powell River) and turn inland onto Duck Lake Forest Service Road. 11.3 kilometres (6.8 mi) along this road you come to the Lang Creek trail marker on the right. Park here.

Hiking Time/Distance: It takes 1 1/4 hours to cover the 5.3-km (3.1-mi) round trip.

Description: Primary as far as the railed lookout over the falls. A steep section takes you right down to the creek where picnic tables are provided.

If you want to see the salmon hatchery across the creek at closer range, go back. Cross the Lang Creek bridge at Duck Lake. From here to the hatchery is 2 km (1.2 mi), taking less than an hour to hike. It can also be driven. The best time of year to see the fry is April to June; to see the salmon return and the workers take the eggs from the fish, go in November or December. The kids can take their fishing rods and try their luck in the creek.

If you continue on The Lang Creek trail you will come out at tiny, peat-bottomed East Lake. Retrace your steps or use the road to complete the circle.

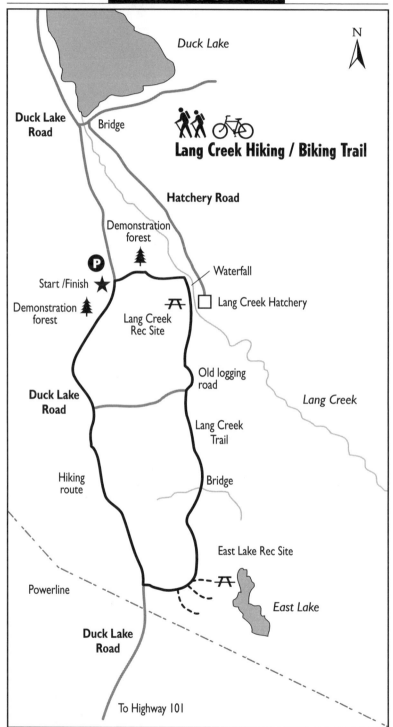

Duck Lake

N

Duck Lake Road

Bridge

Lang Creek Hiking / Biking Trail

Hatchery Road

Demonstration forest

P

Start /Finish

Waterfall

Demonstration forest

Lang Creek Hatchery

Lang Creek Rec Site

Old logging road

Duck Lake Road

Lang Creek

Lang Creek Trail

Hiking route

Bridge

East Lake Rec Site

Powerline

East Lake

Duck Lake Road

To Highway 101

Sweetwater Hiking and Biking Trail

Thick moss, lush ferns and feathery hemlock mark this intermediate rain forest hike. Try it in the morning to catch the sun reflecting on rushing, tumbling Sweetwater Creek. Myriad falls highlight the trail to the summit. This is one of the prettiest forest trails in the district. (See map on page 124.)

Access: Follow Highway 101 23 km (14 mi) north from Saltery Bay or 9.5 km (5.7 mi) south of the Westview ferry terminal in Powell River and turn onto Duck Lake Forest Service Road. Travel 11.5 km (7 mi) to Duck Lake. Turn right at the bridge and go a further 3.6 km (2 mi) to the first intersection. Turn left and continue .4 km (about 250 yards). Park at the pullout.

Hiking Time/Distance: Allow 1 1/2 to 2 hours on the approximately 7 km (4.2 mi) circle trail.

Description: Intermediate. From your car, walk up the old road and follow the trail to the right. Look for the Sweetwater Trail Forest Service sign tacked to a tree. It is approximately 1.5 km (1 mi) to Sweetwater Creek and MacGregor Falls. Fluorescent tree markers guide you along the creek about 1 km (.6 mi) and across an active logging road. Turn left then right just before the bridge. Continue along the trail .5 km (.3 mi) to the summit, then retrace your steps down for a few minutes, go left at the hiker/cycler sign which leads to an old railbed, then out to a road. Turn right, then left at the intersection to return to your car. Cyclists should do this route in reverse and travel the rail bed section only.

CYCLING THE UPPER SUNSHINE COAST

If you are arriving by ferry at Saltery Bay, let all vehicle traffic pass before starting out. New dimensions have been added to cycling in the Powell River District. No longer are you forced to crowd the edge of the highway or eat dust on the logging roads for an afternoon's outing. Several new mountain bike paths have been and are being blazed and several of the hikes listed in the hiking sections also allow mountain bikes. By far the easiest of these trails is the Forestry Museum's Willingdon Beach Trail, a regularly cycled link to the old Townsite. Much longer, but just as scenic, is the 13-km (7.8-mi) Inland Lake Trail.

The new Sunshine Coast Trail has sections that are good for cycling (see the write-up on page 119). It was a dream of the Greenways group to have a cycle path from Saltery Bay to Lund.

When coming from Saltery Bay, one of our most noted cyclists, Phyl Rowell, who pedalled her way across Australia and New Zealand—a 6,400-km (3,800-mile) trip—at 68 years of age, recommends biking Paradise Valley an alternate route for bikers who wish to avoid the highway route to Powell River. Head north from Saltery Bay and turn up Maris Road opposite Myrtle Rocks and turn left on Centennial Drive. The road curves onto Padgett Road,

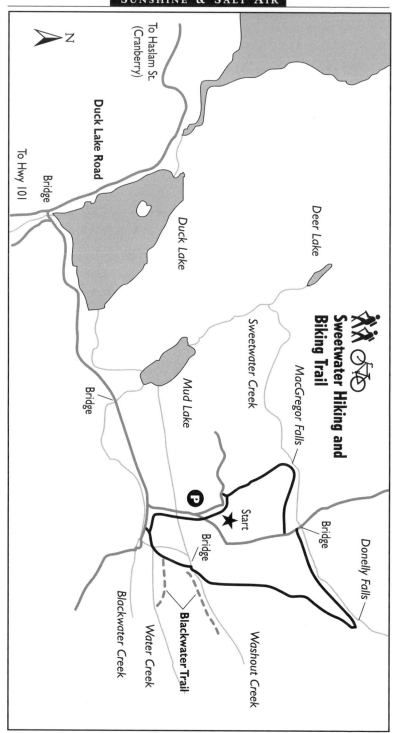

travels through the valley and comes out onto Duncan Street inside the municipality, near the airport.

The Duck Lake area also has a network of hikes, most of which are suitable for mountain biking.

Elephant Lake Bike Loop

This route has a very tough climb but the cyclist is rewarded with spectacular views. It is entirely on logging roads and the highway. (See map on page 126.)

Access: Start from the Saltery Bay ferry terminal or at Highway 101 and the MacMillan Bloedel mainline 12.5 km (7.5 mi) north of the ferry terminal.

Riding Time/Distance: 5–6 hours, 48 km (28.8 mi).

Description: Intermediate/Advanced. The trail is marked with a white biking symbol or a double band of yellow or red paint.

If you are starting from the ferry terminal, follow the Saltery Bay Forest Service Road west for 300 m (330 yd) and take the left fork up the steep section. This steady climb is 8 km (4.8 mi) long. At the fork 1 km (.6 mi) into the climb, keep right. Continue past Rainy Day Lake and the steep, rocky switchback. At the top of the climb you can pause and enjoy the great view of Jervis Inlet. Carry on along the main road to a dangerous intersection at the bottom of a steep downhill. Turn left here (Branch 41) and stay on the main road. Watch carefully for the markers as there are numerous forks in the road. Eight

Roz Voss, Powell River's top mountain biker, is now on the professional circuit.

km (4.8 mi) along you will begin an exciting 10-km (6-mi) descent. At the bottom you will see a gate. Go left at the MacMillan Bloedel mainline and left again on Highway 101 to return to Saltery Bay.

Hazards: There may be active log hauling on these roads. Check with the Forest Service (485-0700) before use.

Blue Trail Bike Loop (Duck Lake Area)

This 1913 railbed has no viewpoint, but is wonderfully cool on a hot summer day. Wide and well defined, it runs alongside a carpet of duff, moss and thick fern. In the fall, masses of mushrooms create interesting photographs, if not good eating.

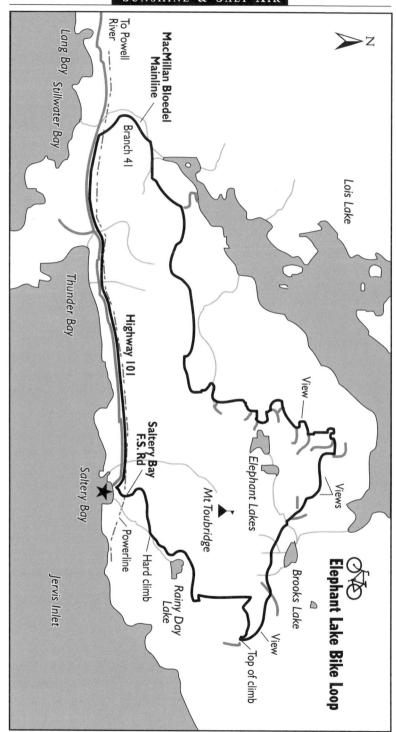

N

To Powell River

Lang Bay
Stillwater Bay

MacMillan Bloedel Mainline

Branch 41

Lois Lake

Highway 101

Thunder Bay

View

Saltery Bay F.S. Rd

Elephant Lakes

Views

Saltery Bay

Mt Toubridge

Powerline

Hard climb

Rainy Day Lake

Brooks Lake

View

Top of climb

Jervis Inlet

Elephant Lake Bike Loop

Access: Follow Highway 101 23 km (14 mi) north from Saltery Bay or 9.5 km (5.7 mi) south of the Westview ferry terminal in Powell River and turn inland onto Duck Lake Forest Service Road. Drive 7.5 km (4.5 mi) and park in the middle of a recently reforested area. The route finishes on the skid road on the left side.

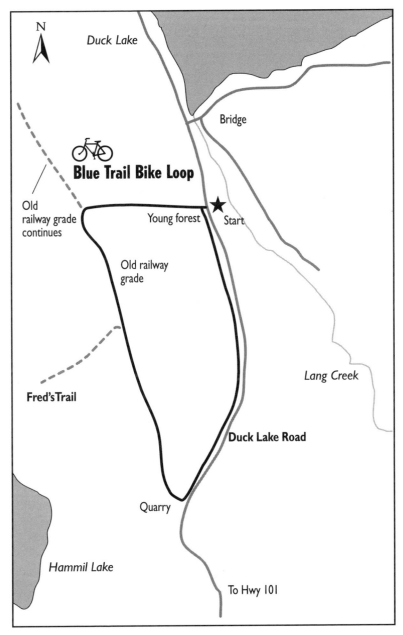

Distance: 3.5 km (2 mi).

Description: Easy, for the most part. The tough part is the downhill section toward the end of the loop. This section should be walked by the inexperienced cyclist.

The route is marked in both directions, but we describe the route clockwise. From the recently cut area backtrack along the road (south) for 1.5 km (1 mi). On the right, just before a small quarry you will see a trail leading into the woods. Follow the trail 15 m (49 ft) to an old rail bed. Turn right and follow it for 1.5 km (1 mi). Turn right on the marked trail and follow the single track 500 m (550 yd) to a recently logged area. Stay on the trail when it becomes a skid road and descend back to the start.

DIVING IN THE SALTERY BAY AREA

The Beach Gardens Hotel, long-time headquarters for all the diving in the Powell River District, no longer gives full service. For air and dive charters call 487-1951. Don's Dive Shop on the government wharf in Westview, 485-6969, is the only full-time professional dive centre in the area, offering charters, lessons, rentals, repairs, sales and air.

As well as the other dives you will find in this book, Kiddie Point on Texada Island conceals a large kelp bed where sea urchins, wolf eels and seals are found. Rebecca Rock, a fabulous reef dive, offers pretty much everything.

Mermaid Cove Shore Dive

This site is the home of Canada's first underwater statue, a 2.7-m (9-ft) bronze mermaid sculpted by Simon Morris. However, the Mermaid is only one of this area's underwater wonders. Saltery Bay is a diver's paradise, as beautiful below the sea as it is above. While your family picnics in the Saltery Bay Mermaid Cove Provincial Park, you can explore the clear depths off the walls beyond the mermaid.

The dive site is wheelchair accessible, and may be the only marine park for disabled divers in Canada.

Access: Travel north on Highway 101 1.8 km (1 mi) from the Saltery Bay ferry terminal. Look for the campsite and park at the top of the path to the beach.

Description: Beginner/Intermediate. Outdoor showers are available for rinsing gear.

Depth: 18.3 m (60 ft) at the Mermaid, 33.5 m (110 ft) off the walls.

Octopus City Shore Dive

This clear water area with sandy bottom makes a good night dive. For added interest a sunken 10-m (33-ft) sailboat shelters a variety of sea life.

**Beautiful Mermaid Cove is home
to Canada's first underwater statue.**

Access: Travel 3.7 km (2.2 mi) north of the Saltery Bay ferry terminal and look for the signs for the Saltery Bay picnic site.

Description: Beginner. Go to the right-hand end of the parking lot and follow the hiking trail until you get to the tree with a dive flag on it. Enter water here and swim out past the rock to the beginning of the sandy bottom. Bear right at approximately 90 degrees until you run into cable. Follow the cable out to the end to the large boulders. This is Octopus City; look for them under the rocks.

Depth: 18.3 m (60 ft).

Hazards: Be sure to bring your dive flag because boats are a real danger here.

CANOEING SOUTH OF POWELL RIVER

The Powell Forest Canoe Route

This magnificent canoe route is one of Powell River's highlights. Whether you take the 3-day mini-route or the full 5- to 7-day trip, you are in for a big treat. The Forest Service maintains and provides dry firewood for 20 recreation sites along the route. The Forest Service also has an excellent and very necessary map of the route available free to anyone interested. Phone (604) 485-0700.

The 12.5-km (7.5-mi) Mini-Canoe Route, with 5 km (3 mi) of portaging, begins at the narrows of Horseshoe and Nanton lakes. The longer main route begins at Lois Lake Forest Service Recreation Site and covers 80 km

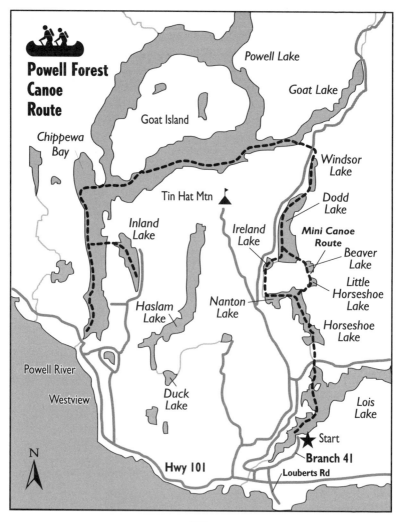

Powell Forest Canoe Route

Powell Lake

Goat Lake

Goat Island

Chippewa Bay

Windsor Lake

Tin Hat Mtn

Dodd Lake

Inland Lake

Ireland Lake

Mini Canoe Route

Beaver Lake

Little Horseshoe Lake

Haslam Lake

Nanton Lake

Horseshoe Lake

Powell River

Westview

Duck Lake

Lois Lake

Start

Branch 41

Louberts Rd

Hwy 101

N

(48 mi) of canoeing and 10.7 km (6.4 mi) of portaging.

Access: While it is possible to make a complete circuit of the main route in either direction, or to begin at any lake, the recommended route is from Lois Lake to Powell Lake. This route avoids going up the 111-m (365-ft) elevation change from Powell Lake to Windsor Lake.

In 1997 new access road to the Lois Lake Forest Recreation Site was opened across from Louberts (Stillwater) Road. Travel 2.4 km (1.4 mi) up this road, then turn right and continue past the fork on right to the Lois Lake Forest Service Recreation Site. Care should be taken as there is active logging truck traffic at various times. Call the Forest Service to check.

Those paddling the Powell Forest Canoe Route
are in for a wonderful adventure. Shown here is Lois Lake.

Lois Lake: This beautiful lake looks serene, but can be treacherous at times as it harbours numerous submerged stumps and snags. Variable winds make the entrance from the lake into the bay hazardous.

Follow the southern shore for approximately 3 km (1.8 mi), then travel due north to the small bay identifiable by two floats. Lois Lake offers an interesting side trip: access to Khartoum (Third) Lake and its Forest Service Recreation Site can be gained by travelling east on Lois Lake to the narrows that lead to Khartoum.

Lois Lake to Horseshoe Lake Portage: It takes about 25 minutes to cover the portage to Horseshoe Lake, a distance of 1.7 km (1 mi).

This is an excellent short trail with some of the best rain forest scenery on the coast. There are four canoe racks along the way with a particularly inviting rack area about 15 minutes in.

The Horseshoe River roars along beside the trail, tumbling over the rocks and falls and filling quiet side pools. There are fish just waiting to be caught in these pools, and two picnic areas offer a spot to fry them up. Near the end, there is a wall of stone where blocks of rock were once quarried for the dam site. Just beyond, a short side trail leads to another canoe launching site.

Horseshoe and Nanton Lakes: Deadheads, driftwood and submerged snags are the hazards of these linked lakes. Paddle along the southern shore of Horseshoe, then bear north and keep to the western shore. There are numerous bays and coves to explore but care should be taken when the winds are whipping up the surface. At the obvious narrows, continue westward into Nanton Lake to the entrance of the connector stream, the upper extension of Horseshoe River. At high water, this stream can be canoed for about 300 m (330 yds), but at low water, canoes will have to be walked through the shallows to the start of the trail. Watch out for soft areas on the lake edge and the stream bottom.

Nanton Lake to Ireland Lake Portage: Along this portage are the remains of an old railway bridge. Large cedar stumps and rusting relics of the early shingle bolt camps recall the days when this area teemed with loggers and the "locies" whistled through the virgin forest. The quiet that nature has restored makes it a good home to many small animals. You may find a dipper bird near his nest in the crevice of the rocks approximately where the old bridge crossed. He's a funny little sooty creature who walks under the water and continually dips his head up and down, looking very "dippy" as he does so.

It takes 40 minutes to cover the 2.4-km (1.4-mi) portage.

This relatively flat path winds along the shore and through the damp cedar valley. Eight canoe racks and two rest areas are provided.

Ireland Lake: Ireland is a small shallow lake about 1 km (.6 mi) in length. There is good fishing along the shores and at the stream mouths. The remains of a railway trestle along the shore can be seen from the Dodd Lake Campsite. Along the path are numerous moss-covered stumps, more reminders of the shingle bolt era.

Picturesque Windsor Lake,
part of an 80-km canoe route that offers paddlers a choice of 20 camping areas.

Ireland Lake to Dodd Lake Portage: This short portage is 820 m (900 yds) long. A few tight corners make manoeuvring difficult for canoes over 4.8 m (16 ft). Two canoe racks are provided and the grade is good all the way. Bridges span the muddy sections and small creek. Even those who relish whitewater thrills are reminded not to canoe the connector stream.

Dodd Lake: This usually calm lake is to be treated with respect. It is subject to sudden wind squalls on warm afternoons. Canoeists can find many little bays on either shore to shelter in until the wind dies down around 5:00 p.m.

Dodd to Windsor Lake Portage: This .7 km (.4 mi) portage follows an old corduroy skid road. The landing at the Dodd Lake side is the original landing site used to supply the early loggers. A rejuvenated 1920s bridge crosses the stream. Two canoe racks are provided.

From Goat Lake, rich green mountains rise steeply skyward.

Windsor Lake: At 196 m (647 ft), cool green Windsor Lake is the highest of the lakes on the circuit. This is a very deep lake, nestled at the base of the mountains.

Windsor Lake to Goat Lake Portage: This portage is just 2.4 km (1.4 mi) long, but its steepness makes it seem much longer. As there is no connector stream between these lakes, this portage is not as scenic as the others. The 111-m (366-ft) drop in elevation from Windsor to Goat Lake necessitates several switchbacks on the lower section of the route. Eleven canoe racks ease the load along the way.

Goat Lake and Goat Island, Powell Lake: From the recreation site, paddle 2 km (1.2 mi) northwest to the narrows and make your way through to Powell Lake. From here, cross to the southern shore of Goat Island and continue about 2.5 km (1.5 mi) to the point of land at the southernmost end of Goat Island. There is now a campsite in this area for your enjoyment.

Chippewa Bay, South Powell Lake and alternate route to Inland Lake: This last portion of the route often causes problems during hot weather, when the northwest wind blows in and out of Chippewa Bay. Although the winds die down in late afternoon, extra care should be taken at all times. From Chippewa Bay, follow the western shore of the lake to the marina, or to the picnic area just before the marina. To avoid the potentially dangerous winds, an alternate portage route to Inland Lake has been opened.

The Forest Service Recreation Site at Inland Lake provides a good spot for parking vehicles while on the canoe route.

KAYAKING THE UPPER SUNSHINE COAST

The most popular and safe areas to paddle include the enticing harbours of Desolation Sound, the Copeland Islands, Savary Island, and four of the lakes of the Canoe Route: Nanton, Dodd, Windsor and Goat.

If you have arrived with your own kayak, listen to the weather forecast for the Strait of Georgia before going out.

If you are new to the sport, know how to self-rescue and participate in the rescue of others before you start out. Two very knowledgable kayak outfits are Powell River Sea Kayak (604-483-2160) and Wolfson Creek Ventures (604-487-1699). Both offer instruction, daily tours and expeditions. With PR Sea Kayak, there are a variety of choices, from a two- to four-hour introductory tour, a six-hour explorer jaunt in Okeover, a visit to an oyster farm where you can sample the tasty delicacies with vino de casa, or a Coast Salish expedition, complete with native lore and a traditional salmon barbeque.

WHERE TO STAY SOUTH OF POWELL RIVER

B&B by the Sea—Southern Comfort. 8711 Hwy 101, Myrtle Point. Phone: 487-1377, toll-free 1-877-711-1377. The ocean's at your doorstep.

Brock's Bayview Retreat Bed and Breakfast. 12717 Hwy 101. Phone: 487-9175. Fax: 487-0099. Peace and privacy on the ocean.

Donkersley Beach Bed and Breakfast. 10201 Douglas Bay Road, (right off Donkersley Road). Phone 487-9215. Self-contained cottage, self-serve breakfast.

Fern Hill Bed and Breakfast. 2744 Zilinski Road. Phone: 487-0644. Self-contained suite on nine secluded acres on Wolfson Creek.

Garnet Rock Ocean Front Mobile Home Park and Campground, 8425 Hwy. 101, Myrtle Point. Phone: 487-9535. Close to Myrtle Point Golf Course.

Hampshire's Country Inn. Bed and Breakfast. Hwy. 101, Lang Bay. Phone: 487-9012 or 487-9011. Panoramic view.

Herondell Bed and Breakfast. Highway 101, Lang Bay. Phone: 487-9528. Next to a tranquil duck pond.

Heartlands Bed and Breakfast. Zilinsky Road. Phone: 487-9942. Fax: 487-4423. Enjoy four-story historic farmhouse on 10 acres, personal adventure tours.

Lang Bay Lifestyles Resort. 2119 Lang Bay Road, Lang Bay. Phone: 487-0111. Oceanside units with kitchenettes.

Ocean Beach Lodge Bed and Breakfast. 1297 Scotch Fir Road, Lang Bay (off Loubert Road). Phone: 487-9299. Beautiful waterfront location.

Oceanside RV Park. 80-8063 Hwy. 101, Myrtle Point. Phone: 485-2435, Toll Free: 1-888-771-7776. Motel units and RV rental.

Seabreeze Resort. Seabreeze Road. Phone/fax: 487-9534. Self-contained cottages.

Seashore Bed and Breakfast. 9441 Stittle Road, Black Point (off highway at Reave Road). Phone: 487-0190. Highbank waterfront with a small cabin on beach.

Tanglewood Bed and Breakfast, Duck Lake Road, Myrtle Point, Phone 487-0535. Trail ride lessons available.

DINING OUT SOUTH OF POWELL RIVER

Eagles Landing Bistro, 2365 Lang Bay Road, 487-1050. Full menu, great ribs. $$$

Myrtle Point Golf Club, 2865 McCausland, 487-4653. $$

POWELL RIVER

I t is a 31.9-km (19-mi) drive from Saltery Bay to the Westview ferry terminal in Powell River where the ferry crosses to Comox on Vancouver Island. This is where many travellers say goodbye to Highway 101; and in doing so, they miss some of the more spectacular views and interesting historic sites on the Sunshine Coast.

Leave us if you must!—but first, consider taking a later ferry, because the terminal is just 30 km (18 mi) south of scenic Lund where Highway 101 ends at the dock. And there's lots to see along the way.

Westview is the commercial centre of Powell River and offers a pleasant main street of small shops, restaurants and two large malls. As you continue north from the terminal turnoff, the new Visitors Infocentre is on the right at .6 km (.4 mi), just past the Gibsons Crossing shops.

Paddling is a great way to explore the Sunshine Coast.

As you cross Abbotsford Street you'll have the feeling that you're leaving town, but even then you will see the museum on your right and the Willingdon Beach park on the left. But you're not leaving town, you're driving to its historic centre just 3 km (1.8 mi) beyond, the pride and joy of local heritage buffs, the Powell River Townsite.

Built early in the century by the Powell River Paper Company, the Townsite is one of Canada's best-preserved examples of a classic company town.

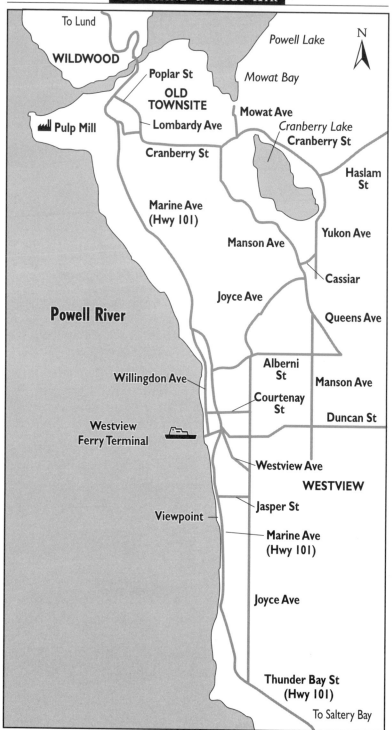

To Lund

Powell Lake

N

WILDWOOD

Poplar St

Mowat Bay

OLD TOWNSITE

Mowat Ave

Cranberry Lake

Cranberry St

Pulp Mill

Lombardy Ave

Cranberry St

Haslam St

Marine Ave (Hwy 101)

Manson Ave

Yukon Ave

Powell River

Joyce Ave

Cassiar

Queens Ave

Willingdon Ave

Alberni St

Manson Ave

Courtenay St

Westview Ferry Terminal

Duncan St

Westview Ave

WESTVIEW

Viewpoint

Jasper St

Marine Ave (Hwy 101)

Joyce Ave

Thunder Bay St (Hwy 101)

To Saltery Bay

*An aerial view of the MacMillan Bloedel pulp mill
and Westview with Texada Island behind.*

On the way into town, the MacMillan Bloedel viewpoint overlooks the still very active mill and the Townsite's old commercial core. In the foreground are company offices with the second community centre, Dwight Hall, behind. Up the hill to the right, near the churches, is the Patricia Theatre, said to be the oldest operating movie theatre business in BC. Turning to the hillside above, you can admire some of the Townsite's finer old homes. Note in particular the well-built homes across the street on the second block, which was known as "Bosses' Row."

The Townsite has much to offer: the mill itself, which offers tours during the summer, Dwight Hall, the Patricia Theatre and much more. The legacy of 60 to 80 years of landscaping can be seen everywhere, in thriving

DR. ISRAEL WOOD POWELL

In 1880, Captain Verle Orlebar of the surveying ship HMS *Rocket* charted the river and waterfall which lay between Jervis Inlet and Desolation Sound. He named them in honour of one of the *Rocket's* passengers, Dr. Israel Wood Powell, who at the time was Superintendent of Indian Affairs for British Columbia. To our knowledge, Powell never set foot on the shores which bear his name, but he distinguished himself in other ways: as the first president of the BC Medical Association, and as a strong voice for keeping BC in confederation with the Canadas when it appeared that it may become a US territory.

A restored townsite heritage building from 1912.

THE HISTORIC TOWNSITE OF POWELL RIVER

In 1995, the federal government designated the townsite of Powell River the first official "Heritage District" west of the Maritimes. This was a coup for the Townsite Heritage Society, which had been campaigning for years to preserve this unique site. The Powell River Company—founded by three Minnesota men, Dwight and Anson Brooks and M. Joseph Scanlon—carved the townsite out of the wilderness between 1911 and 1930. The company built one of the first wood pulp and paper mills in western Canada and on April 12, 1912, the first newsprint rolled off its machines.

The owners of the Powell River Company hoped to build a model company town that would instill pride in its workers. The Townsite plan was carefully laid out, with the utility lines in the back alleys and trees lining the streets. Worker-tenants were provided with a school, library, hospital, churches, athletic fields, tennis courts, lawn bowling and a department store, all maintained by the ever-present Townsite Gang. Unlike other company towns, this one encouraged independent businesses. Company employees took part in annual garden contests, and the Townsite became known as a "Garden City." Fitness was encouraged and the company gave good athletes priority in its hiring policy. They kept an athletic director, as well as the town librarian, on the payroll.

With two churches, the place was planned to nurture the whole man. Nor was man's thirst overlooked, with a busy watering hole, the Rodmay Hotel, strategically located across from the mill gates. Almost as much a Powell River Landmark as the Hulks, the Rodmay was built in 1911 as the 30-room Powell River Hotel, owned by Andrew McKinney, and still does a roaring business between shifts.

Between 1919 and 1931, almost all the new buildings in the Townsite were designed by Townsite Manager John McIntyre. An example is the Bank of Montreal at the corner of Ash and Walnut. Before 1931, the Powell River Company dealt solely with the Bank of Commerce (no longer standing). When the Commerce refused the Company a loan to complete their #7 paper machine and the Lois River Dam project, the officers went to the Commerce's opposition with a deal: the company would build a handsome bank and manager's apartment if the bank would loan the required money. It did, the money was borrowed and a new Tudor Revival bank building was added to the community—right across the street from the Bank of Commerce!

All of the Townsite houses were designed to be moved, making the Townsite a "temporary town." Old-timers claim this gave the company a tax advantage. The oldest of these "temporary" homes celebrated their eightieth birthdays between 1991 and 1997, and still sport strong, firm lines.

The seven cottages on the inland side of Sycamore Street were built starting in 1911. It is believed they were designed by master builder George Ingemann of Minnesota, Townsite Manager until 1916. The houses with the bell-curved roofs all pre-date 1916. The former Powell River Company Guest House on Marine Avenue was originally built for the first director of the company, Norman Lang, in 1911.

Ever progressive, the Powell River Company installed crank telephones in the mill and in department managers' homes from 1910 to 1912. Powell River hooked up BC's first dial phones in 1921 and BC's first radiotelephone circuit in 1930. On the lower side of Walnut, behind a modern facade, is the 1931 Northwest Telephone Building.

A logging locomotive used to rumble through the Townsite on its way to Michigan Landing (Willingdon Beach). The track was pulled up in 1926 and the railbed, sometimes still referred to as Lover's Lane, is now the home of the Forestry Museum's display of logging relics.

In the late 1990s, 97 percent of the Townsite buildings were original. A stroll through the site provides the visitor with a rare opportunity to travel back in time to visit a classic company town.

rhododendron, oak, arbutus, cedars and on the way into town, even an enormous monkey puzzle tree.

Powell River Museum, Archives and Art Gallery

Don't miss the Museum across from Willingdon Beach. This well-established regional collection offers something for everyone. The octagonal building features First Nations exhibits, a Powell River Company mill display and a reproduction of the cabin occupied by "Billy Goat" Smith, a legendary local pioneer who lived with domestic goats.

In the Centennial building next door are the Archives, and the Art Gallery featuring the art and photography of local artists.

The Rodmay Hotel showing the 1924 addition.

Sam Sing

Sam Sing was Powell River Townsite's first land merchant. He operated a laundry and small store on Waterfront Street c. 1907–09, and a

MACMILLAN BLOEDEL VIEWPOINT

This viewpoint overlooking the gargantuan MacMillan Bloedel pulp mill offers a panoramic view of the old Powell River business district, dating back to the era when it was a model company town. On the left are two totem poles created by renowned carver Mungo Martin in Kingcome Inlet in the 1920s, and restored in 1987 by local carver Jackie Timothy. On the right is an enormous valve from the mill foundry. It is on the water below, however, that you will see one of the most unusual sights on the coast.

Protecting the mill's log pond from wave action is the world's largest breakwater of floating ships. Known as "The Hulks," it is made up of concrete World War II supply ships, which replaced the wooden hulls that were brought here in 1930. At certain times of the year, even from the MacMillan Bloedel viewpoint, you can hear a tremendous racket coming from the direction of the hulks. If you have binoculars you'll be able to see where the noise is coming from—sea lions on the log booms, honking and barking at each other on this stopover from their travels up and down the coast. As the shore nearby is MacMillan Bloedel property, frequented by logging trucks and other heavy equipment, it's not recommended that you try to get down for a closer look. The pulp mill offers tours from June until September to show visitors the pond, the Hulks, and other fascinating aspects of the mill's operation.

On the hillside above the viewpoint is the residential section of the old company townsite, featuring a two-block row of well-built homes known for obvious reasons as "Bosses' Row"—although one of the more imposing edifices was actually occupied by a Dr. Lyon.

tent store in 1910, and tallied his customers' purchases on an abacus, moving the cents beads one way, the dollars the other. It is told that when the mill payroll was lost one day, the company went to him to see if he would buy some land so they could pay their employees. He agreed, choosing a lot in the centre of town to erect a store and restaurant. The payroll was found, but Sam Sing wouldn't sell the land back. He erected the Sing Lee Block in 1912, finally sold it to the company in 1923 and reopened a similar business block at the Shinglemill, near the entrance to the river on Powell Lake.

Sing started a truck garden in Wildwood between Lund Street and Columbia and later expanded his Chinese Gardens to the farm at the end of King Street. He sold the fresh produce in his grocery stores. With Sam Sing around, you didn't have to owe your soul to the company store.

He and his wife raised five sons and two daughters. Two sons, Henry and Paul, carried on the family businesses with Penny Profit and Fairway Food Market. Another son, Tom, operated Westview Autobody Shop, and today, Sam's grandson Jack continues to serve Powell River with his Westview Radiators repair shop, almost a century after his grandfather opened his laundry and store. They are the only family to cater to Powell River's citizens continuously for that length of time.

Boat Day

While most coastal communities had one Boat Day a week, in 1923 Powell River had six. The town boasted a service that was the envy of every logging camp and cannery stop along the coast. Not only were they serviced by the "Upcoast street-car," the Union steamship, but also by Canadian Pacific, Canadian National, Grand Trunk Pacific, Waterhouse (later Union-Waterhouse) and, after World War II, the faster diesel boats of the Gulf Lines.

The local businessman never had it better. He could board Canadian Pacific's SS *Charmer*, or later the SS *Princess Mary* at eleven at night, be rocked to sleep in a comfortable stateroom, and after a first class breakfast with fresh linen and silverware, walk down the gangplank into downtown Vancouver.

With the advent of the car came change, but even then, until the fifties the best a family could do was to book one of the *Princess Mary's* six precious car spaces a half year in advance, then hope that when it came time for them to start on their holiday, they would not be bumped to accommodate an extra large shipment of paper.

The dream of a road to Vancouver became compelling, but it wasn't until after World War II, when more money and more cars were in circulation, that the dream began to become reality.

In 1947, Powell River had more cars per capita per mile of road than any other town in Canada. As the main road only stretched from Stillwater to Lund, residents were bursting to be able to drive the open highway beyond Vancouver—any day they pleased.

> **"DOC" HENDERSON**
>
> **P**owell River's first practising physician, Dr. Andrew Henderson, came to Powell River as a favour to his Minnesota friends, Brooks and Scanlon, owners of the Powell River Company. Henderson had served during the Riel Rebellion and had been Calgary's first doctor before heading west to the coast. In 1910, he and the company started the first medical plan in British Columbia. Each employee paid $1 per month for all their medical needs, including their wives' pregnancies, although oddly enough the plan did not cover dependents until the late 1940s. In 1913 the town's first hospital, St. Luke's, was built for Dr. Henderson. It is now the Kenmar Building on the corner of Walnut and Arbutus.

Following a fire in Toronto harbour in 1949, a new regulation required sprinkler systems on all passenger boats, which helped speed the demise of the steamships. Most of them were getting too old to justify the expensive refit, so one by one they were taken off their runs.

The SS Prince George arriving at the new Westview wharf in 1946.

With the opening of the airport in 1952, there was more competition for the fading ships. Then, in 1954, the Black Ball Ferries finally linked the community by road to the rest of the province with the MV *Quillayute*. A regular bus route was established to Vancouver and the remaining passenger ship sailings dropped off. In 1958, the last boat, the SS *Prince George* with three short blasts of her whistle, made its final run, signalling the end of the era.

Cranberry—Powell River's first suburb

Named for the bog fruit that grows at the southern end of the lake, Cranberry Lake, as the village used to be called, was the first suburb of the Powell River townsite.

Three ambitious men, George Smarge, Magnes Olson and George McFall, cleared the trees and laid the planks that became the Cranberry Road in 1913, but it wasn't until 1921, when the government subdivided Crown Land around the lake and held a drawing for World War I veterans, that Cranberry blossomed. However, even though lots drawn could be purchased for one dollar, many of the vets resold their lots for a pittance, not deeming them fit for a homesite! In 1946, following World War II, the government again accommodated veterans by building homes on half acres and selling them for $6,000 to returning soldiers. Panoramic views of the surrounding area can be seen by hiking up nearby Valentine Mountain.

While in the area, it is well worth stopping to visit Mitchell Bros., a landmark heritage general store. Its friendly service and eclectic stock will take you back to the days when grocers sold everything from green beans to gumboots. Nearby Cranberry Pottery is the source of the unique Cranberry and Blackberry patterns.

Lindsay Park is located on Cranberry Lake but the lake has been known to foster the parasite that causes "swimmer's itch." Mowat Bay

Municipal Park is the recommended area for swimming and was the location of a shingle mill from 1915 to 1919. The park is a favourite of locals and tourists alike. There are two hikes from the park, a fairly short one that heads over the hill toward the Shinglemill Restaurant and Pub, and a tougher one that leads into Haywire Bay, the Regional District campground.

Beloved by the birds and water lilies, Cranberry Lake is also a winter wonderland if the temperature drops below the freezing point for several weeks—as it tends to do every few years. Since 1911, Powell Riverites have been skating beneath the stars, toasting hot dogs and warming their hands on lakeshore bonfires. Visitors may want to visit the Haslam Lake reservoir,

THE MASTER PHOTOGRAPHER

Rod LeMay trained in Rome as a sculptor and lived in Montreal before arriving in Powell River in 1907. He photographed the river and falls before the mill was even a dream, showing his artistic training in his romantic landscape compositions. After Brooks and Scanlon arrived, they hired him to photograph the progress of the dam and mill construction as well as the Townsite growth. With his Romera 6 view camera he expertly recorded the early town on large glass negatives.

In the early twenties, he made his home in Wildwood on 5th Avenue. It was renamed LeMay Avenue in his honour but changed to Lois Street in 1959. Later he resided on King Street until declining health forced him to move into Vancouver, where he died in 1949.

Rod LeMay's classic 1908 photo of the falls on Powell River before construction of the dam.

though the lake is closed to swimmers and campers. Haslam Street leads to a variety of hiking treats including the Gallagher Hill hike and the Inland Lake trails. Campsites are available at both Inland Lake and Haywire Bay.

Logger Sports

This annual World Championship event, held in July, attracts the best loggers from all over the Pacific Northwest in a wide array of entertaining events. Don't miss this one if you're in town.

Sea Fair Festival

The three-day event, held in August, includes a Saturday morning parade, a fly-past of aircraft old and new, a visit of naval ships, food and craft booths, and the highlight of the festival, Saturday night fireworks over the water. Don't miss the sidewinder rodeo. Sidewinders are tiny, tippy, tough and powerful boats used to "round up" logs into booms.

Kathaumixw

Kathaumixw (pronounced *Ka-thou-mew*) is a native word meaning "the gathering of different peoples."

Kathaumixw, Powell River's biannual choral festival,
draws choirs from all over the world.

Kathaumixw, the International Choral Festival, began in 1984 with nine choirs. Originally conceived by Don James, Director of the Powell River Academy of Music, Dal Matterson and Rob Sabine, it has grown into a major international event. In 1996, 30 choirs came from 17 countries on 5 continents.

Choirs all over the world send audition tapes for a place in the biannual competition. Selected choirs perform at two concerts, with the massed choirs performing at the opening and closing ceremonies.

Even if the choirs don't go home with trophies, they always take back a multitude of memories: informal games at Willingdon Beach, barbecues with their host families, new friendships, impromptu concerts, beach parties, inspiring opening nights and heartwarming closing ceremonies. Old-timers feel Kathaumixw recaptures the early community spirit of Powell River.

For more information on Kathaumixw, call the Academy of Music at (604) 483-3346 or fax (604) 483-3383.

Anne Cameron

Anne Cameron is by far the most prominent and prolific writer in the Powell River district. Although we can't claim her as home-grown—she was brought up on Vancouver Island—she has been with us for more than a decade.

She has been writing since she was very young, producing best-selling novels, legends, poems and film scripts. *Dreamspeaker*, a 1979 film, took seven Canadian film awards, and *Daughters of Copper Woman* has sold over 200,000 copies in a country where 5,000 is considered a best-seller.

She lives with her partner Eleanor on a farm in the area, and has five grown children and seven grandchildren.

Luke Raffin

Luke Raffin (*Ra-feen*), 1990 Artist of the Year for Ducks Unlimited, was born and raised in northern Italy. He was only twelve in 1967 when he arrived in Powell River and, inspired by the beauty of the west coast, began to paint. At the

Author Anne Cameron at home in 1996.

Ontario College of Art in Toronto, he learned how to use egg tempera to produce the fine detail and richness of colour and tone that characterize his work.

He began painting wildlife in 1976, initially concentrating on the bird or animal itself, much later adding a realistic background to first "The Steller's Jay" and then "The Osprey." Now he adds a full background to each of the eight paintings he does a year. In fact, one of his paintings, of Shelter Point on Texada Island at low tide, is all landscape (1996). The eagle is only incidental to the scene.

Luke Raffin lives in Powell River with his wife Miguelle and children Nicholas and Christy. Stop by his gallery across the street from Gibsons Crossing to appreciate the depth and realism in his many fine works.

Texada Island

Texada is the large island that parallels, a few miles offshore, much of the upper Sunshine Coast. The island was first charted by the Spaniards in 1791, although it is believed they never came ashore. A Native legend says that the island rose from the sea and will one day return to the sea. The early aboriginals fished its rivers but refused to stay overnight for fear the island would sink while they slept.

Mineral-rich Texada held no such fear for the white men who explored and stayed to mine the iron, limestone, copper, silver and even gold. From the first iron mine in 1880 to the peak of mining activity when 7 mines operated at once, Texada was a stockbroker's dream and nightmare. Mine names like "Copper King," "The Butterfly" and "Golden Slipper" reflect Texada's history—as rich as her mines. Today the limestone quarries continue to produce a living for many of the island's 1,100 year-round residents.

Texada Island is served by several ferries each day.

Wildwood to Sliammon

After passing through the Townsite, the road leads north. If you follow the signs to Sliammon and Lund, a right turn takes you along Powell River itself. On the left, picturesque old boathouses, connected by a newly planked boardwalk, offer a closeup of the river's clear waters, cruising Canada geese and other waterfowl, and a great full-length view of North America's shortest river (1.2 km/.7 mi).

CHOCOLATE LILY
(Fritillaria lanceolata)

Commonly called "rice root" because the immature bulbs resemble rice, this delicate lily blooms in spring and early summer. One of the places you can look at but not pick these dark beauties is on Myrtle Rocks and Scout Mountain on the upper Sunshine Coast.

Continue on Highway 101, cross the Wildwood Bridge, pass the road to the Shinglemill restaurant and marina, and begin the S-curve up to Wildwood. Going up the hill reveals a good view of Powell Lake, hardly altered since the first Natives slipped their dugout canoes into the water to fish for kokanee and rainbow and cutthroat trout. This immensely deep (416 m/1,370 ft) lake was once an inlet of the sea. Carved from the Coast Mountains during the Ice Age, it was landlocked when the glaciers receded and it became a freshwater lake, although a layer of ancient (at least 7,300 years old) sea water has been discovered 150 m (500 ft) below its surface. Note the sign for the Switchback Trail, a new, well-marked addition to Powell River's hikes, which takes an hour to complete.

For almost fifty years, four rows of houses overlooked the lake from this bank, forming the Shinglemill community. Jamison's sawmill stood on the shore to the left. Small runabouts carried their owners out for a day's fishing or to holiday float houses around the lake. By the early sixties, the buildings were all gone, but the marina still flourishes and the Shinglemill Bistro and Pub display wonderful old photos.

As you wind up the hill, the large home on your right, once owned by Sam Sing, had its chimney turned right around in the 1946 earthquake.

Wildwood, as the name suggests, was nothing but wooded wilderness before it was logged. Many wind-falls made travelling difficult. As in most areas of the district, the loggers preceded the white pioneers, and as early as 1900 the BC Mills, Timber and Trading Company (Hastings Mill) ran 4 km (2.5 mi) of track from today's settled area of Wildwood to the log dumping ground south of Sliammon Creek mouth.

Jim Springer, one of Wildwood's first pioneers, logged with this outfit from 1902 until it pulled out in 1904. He came again in 1907 to work for the Michigan and Puget Sound Logging outfit and this time he stayed. He had also logged on the Townsite in 1883–84 with the Moodyville Saw Company. Years

Canada geese wintering on a farm in the Black Point area.

later, he talked of how he could have bought the whole Townsite for a song—a favourite refrain of the old-timers.

The rich soil of the area—when it was finally reached beneath the logging debris—was a boon to early farmers and gardeners. Many of our immigrants from Italy chose to live in this area, although Wildwood could never truly be termed "Little Italy" as there were just as many other nationalities living alongside them.

Sunset Park at the foot of Scout Mountain is one of the community's attractions, as is the mountain itself. To find it, turn right on King Street and right again on Lois and go up the hill.

Continuing on the highway, now called Lund Street, you will come to the neighbourhood watering hole, the Red Lion Pub at the corner of Sutherland and Lund Street. A hike on the mountain (page 148), followed by a refreshing drink at the Red Lion, makes any sunny afternoon a treat.

If you would like to hike to Third Mile Bay or the Sliammon Lakes, turn right at Sutherland Avenue and follow it to the end (as the last portion is not paved it appears to be a different road, but it isn't). As the Sliammon Lake access tends to change from year to year, pick up a trail sheet at the Visitors' Bureau on Marine in Westview for either hike.

About a mile from the Red Lion Pub, just off the highway on your left, is Gibsons Beach Park. The road now divides the MacMillan Bloedel experimental poplar farm. The fast-growing poplars may someday provide an alternative to the use of our coniferous forests for pulp and paper use. This poplar farm borders on Sliammon Village.

HIKES IN THE POWELL RIVER AREA

Valentine Mountain

This hike should take priority if your time in the district is limited. It offers the best view and the greatest variety of plant life for the least amount of exertion. Not that you won't exert yourself climbing the ninety or so railed steps to the top.

On this trail you may hear grouse hooting in the shrubbery as well as the trills of smaller bird life and the scrambling of squirrels. Some of the many varieties of plant life gracing the rock ledges are creeping juniper, western serviceberry, yellow violet, honeysuckle, blue-eyed Mary, wild strawberries, Oregon grape, salal and huckleberry.

Access: From the Westview ferry terminal follow Marine (Hwy 101) north to the traffic light at Alberni Street. Turn right up Alberni to Manson Avenue and follow Manson to its end where it meets Cranberry Street. Turn left here, and right at Crown Avenue, just this side of the cemetery. Drive to

From Valentine Mountain
a spectacular vista unfolds.

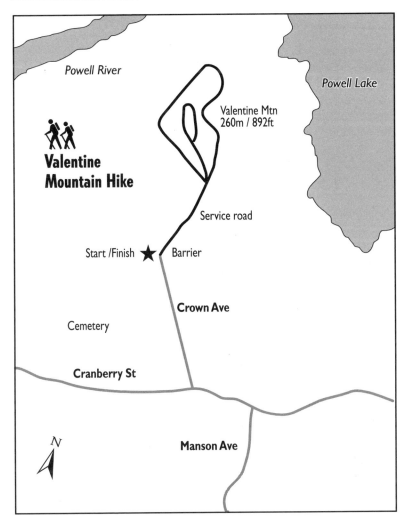

Powell River

Powell Lake

Valentine Mtn
260m / 892ft

**Valentine
Mountain Hike**

Service road

Start /Finish ★ Barrier

Crown Ave

Cemetery

Cranberry St

N

Manson Ave

the parking lot in front of the barrier.

Hiking Time/Distance: It's just 12 short minutes to the top, but allow yourself 45 minutes to explore. The hike up is less than .6 km (.4 mi), but you can cover three times that distance before you reach your car again.

Description: Primary to Intermediate. The steep but short trek leads to the southwestern bluff overlooking Malaspina Strait. Take a leisurely stroll around the trails at the summit. There are three secluded picnic tables so pack a lunch and enjoy four distinct views of the upper Sunshine Coast and the islands: Texada, left; Harwood, centre; Savary from the southwest summit with Vancouver Island in the background; Cortes Island beyond Savary. Westview is to your right. The interesting Tudor building in the townsite is the old courthouse.

A short walk through the kinnikinnick takes you to the east side of Valentine overlooking Mowat Bay and Cranberry Lake on the south, and the first third of Powell Lake to the north. Still travelling counterclockwise, you can see more of Powell Lake with the beautiful snow-crested mountains beyond. Farther along the trail, the northwestern view takes in the Powell Lake Marina, the Kinsmen Park, One Mile Bay, a patch of Wildwood, and Scout Mountain looming up from the park.

Hazards: The trails often skirt the edge of the mountain, so watch that slippery moss, and your youngsters.

Confederation Lake Hike

Parts of this hike look down over Inland Lake and Powell Lake. The main attraction when you arrive at the 600-m (2,000-ft) level is the excellent view of Beartooth Mountain and surrounding range. When the weather is good you can also see Tin Hat Mountain. The level area on the southwest section of the lake is great for picnicking. Keep your eyes open as there is a

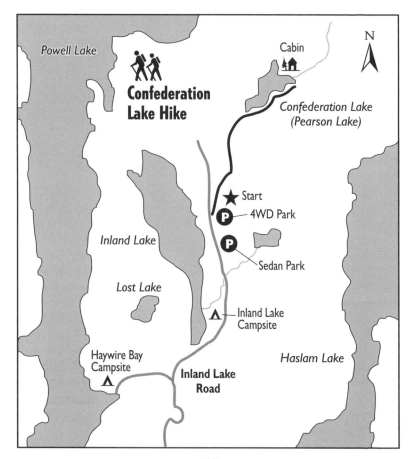

possibility of finding a patch of ladyslipper or the tiny calypso orchids at the top. Colonies of Venus flytrap, another interesting species, can also be found in the area around the lake.

Hiking Time/Distance: It takes 4–6 hours to hike the 12-km (7.2-mi) round trip.

Access: From the Westview ferry terminal follow Marine (Hwy 101) north to the traffic light at Alberni Street. Turn right up Alberni to Manson Avenue; turn left and follow it to Cassiar Street, turn right on Cassiar, which runs into Yukon, and follow Yukon to Haslam Street. Turn right on Haslam and continue to the first junction and take the left branch, Inland Lake Road. Travel this forestry road past the turnoffs to Haywire Bay and Inland Lake Campsites. Just a stone's throw past the Inland Lake Campsite, a road leads to the right. Turn right and drive 2 km (1.2 mi) to the parking pull-off if you don't have four-wheel drive or you are worried about your vehicle; otherwise you can drive another kilometre to another fork in the road.

Description: Intermediate to Advanced. Pick a bright sunny morning in late July to mid-August for the best rewards on this hike and plan to make it an all-day adventure.

Continue on foot up the right fork, angling up the mountain. This washed-out road narrows to a trail. It climbs gently up the foothill of Mt. Mahoney, overlooking Inland (Loon) Lake and Powell Lake beyond. The Bunster Hills and Vancouver Island are in the distance.

A new wooden ramp and set of steps replaces the short rope that used to help you up the steep bank. From here, tin markers and blazes on the trees mark the groomed trail that winds through the old-growth forest.

A rough trail leads to the Forest Service

HAIRY MANZANITA

The Hairy Manzanita (*Arctostaphylos columbiana*) shrub, like the Arbutus tree, is exclusive to the Gulf Island Biotic Zone, and even here, is only found on sunny, rocky slopes and bluffs. True to its name, the twigs and young leaves are very hairy, the limbs are strikingly crooked and its reddish-orange colouring is not unlike the arbutus.

In May, the white flowers resemble those of the arbutus, with which the shrub is often found. The blackish-red mealy berries are edible and were traditionally gathered by Indians to be eaten either raw or cooked.

Discovering the Manzanita on the way to the top of Pender Hill is one of the rewards of the climb. The shrub also grows around Sakinaw Lake and Valentine Mountain.

cabin and outhouse on the far side of the lake, then winds down to Fiddlehead Farm on Powell Lake. Plans are in the works by the Forest Service to build a trail to the ridge of Mt. Mahoney 1,050-m (3,500-ft) level.

Mowat Bay to Powell Lake Shinglemill Hike

This cool mountain trail is perfect after a hot afternoon at the Mowat Bay beach, or beautiful in the golden fall. A heavy frost on the foliage and path makes a sunny winter afternoon extra special. Springtime adds its own delights to this year-round trail that ends steeply at the road, then follows an old logging rail bed on the shore of the lake.

Crowded along the lower trail are majestic old-growth firs that survived the forest fire that devastated the mountainside in 1918. Near the end of the trail look for a shrub that flowers in the summer, *Buddleia arbour*, "Purple Delight."

The Shinglemill Restaurant and Pub display numerous photos of the early settlement on the shore of Powell Lake. The Shinglemill, as the area was called, had houses up the bank and a laundry, store and hotel until 1961.

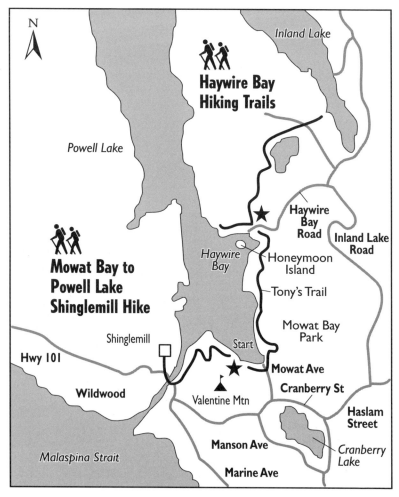

The burners of the shingle mill glowed in the night for almost fifty years.

Access: From the Westview ferry terminal follow Marine (Hwy 101) north to the traffic light at Alberni Street. Turn right up Alberni, then left on Manson Avenue until Manson ends in a "T." Turn right onto Cranberry Street and make your first left onto Mowat Avenue. Park at the beach at the end of Mowat.

Hiking Time/Distance: It takes 25 minutes to hike the 1-km (.6-mi) trail over the mountain and another 10 minutes to reach the Shinglemill. You may want to do this hike with a friend, each taking a vehicle to the beginning/end of the trail.

Description: The hike begins near the lake on the left-hand side. Watch for six steps up the side of the mountain, an old alder and an ancient maple. There are two routes, one steeper than the other. If you want the easier hike, take the right-hand path at the first fork. Coming out of the trail, you reach the logging road, turn right and walk past the shingle bolt operation. At the bottom of the hill, make a sharp left turn and hike along the lake to Marine (Hwy. 101) and the Wildwood Bridge, cross the bridge and take the lower road to the Shinglemill.

Haywire Bay Hiking Trails

A number of first-growth fir are to be seen along the path—giants that somehow escaped destruction in a forest fire. For a time the trail runs alongside Lost Lake, a small mountain lake. (See map on previous page.)

Access: From the Westview ferry terminal follow Marine (Hwy 101) north to the traffic light at Alberni Street. Turn right up Alberni to Manson Avenue, turn left and follow it to Cassiar Street, turn right on Cassiar, which runs into Yukon, and follow Yukon to Haslam Street. Turn right on Haslam and continue to the first junction and take the left branch, Inland Lake Road. Follow the signs to the Haywire Bay Regional District campsite.

During the off-season, vehicle access to the campsite may be blocked by a gate across the road, in which case park here and add another 15 minutes to your hiking time.

The Haywire Bay covered eating area is just a swim away from Honeymoon Island.

Description: There are two good hikes at Haywire Bay. Allow about 35 minutes for the easy 2-km (1.2-mi) hike along a pretty path that introduces you to all the bay has to offer. If you are newlyweds, Honeymoon Island off the campsite may be all you are interested in, but there is also a good swimming beach.

The long hike is rated intermediate and follows the 4-km (2.4-mi) trail from Haywire Bay to Inland Lake. It takes about 4 hours return. It is challenging and travels up steep hills and down into gullies and up and down again.

Inland (Loon) Lake Wheelchair, Hiking and Biking Trails

This wonderful woodland path was winner of the 1989 Premier's Award for Excellence in Accessible Design. This one is a must! Although it is an award-winning trail for the disabled, and plans are in the works to make it better for the visually impaired, it is extremely popular with everyone. It has improved since its 1983 beginnings to include a totem pole by renowned local carver Jackie Timothy and 13 smaller carvings by Sechelt carver Terry Chapman. For a donation, an interpretive guide is available from the caretaker on site from April to September. The guided hike covers 18 stops of interest, details the logging history of the lake, identifies wildlife, trees and plants and includes fishing and camping information.

On a warm summer's day, you can go for swims between spells of hiking, and tables are provided along the path for picnic lunches. Most tables are adapted for wheelchair use. Tent sites are available and a small cabin with wheelchair accessibility offers three rustic bunks for the disabled. Firewood is provided.

If it's fish you're after, you can walk or wheel yourself up to one of 6 special fishing docks and enjoy a morning's fishing. This quiet lake is reputed to give up 5- to 6-pound trout.

Inviting Inland Lake offers fishing, swimming and a 13 km hike.

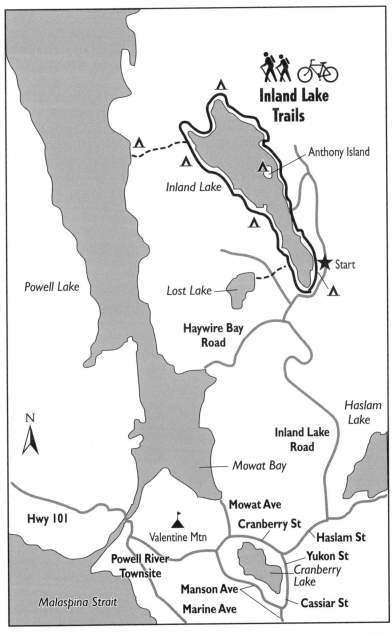

Inland Lake Trails

Anthony Island

Inland Lake

Powell Lake

Lost Lake

★ Start

Haywire Bay Road

Haslam Lake

N

Inland Lake Road

Mowat Bay

Mowat Ave

Cranberry St

Hwy 101

Valentine Mtn

Haslam St

Yukon St

Cranberry Lake

Powell River Townsite

Manson Ave

Marine Ave

Cassiar St

Malaspina Strait

Access: From the Westview ferry terminal follow Marine (Hwy 101) north to the traffic light at Alberni Street. Turn right up Alberni to Manson Avenue, turn left and follow it to Cassiar Street, turn right on Cassiar, which runs into Yukon, and follow Yukon to Haslam Street. Turn right on Haslam and continue to the first junction and take the left branch, Inland Lake Road.

Continue on to the turnoff for the Inland Lake Forest Service Recreation Site.

Hiking Time/Distance: It takes 4 to 6 hours to make your way completely around the lake (13 km/7.8 mi)—4 if you really hike it, and 6 if you stop for lunch and explore the side trails to Powell Lake and Lost Lake. It takes about 30 minutes return to do each of these short trails.

Description: Intermediate. Although very flat (and great for cycling!), the trail is long if you attempt the whole route without being in shape—whether hiking or via wheelchair. Wheelchair athletes would have no difficulty. Don't let this discourage you though, as an hour's walk in a northern direction, right from the campsite, treats you to the sights and sounds of real wilderness country where tall cedars shade the forest trail. Each end is as different as its predominant trees, with the southern portion more like a pretty path that follows the edge of the lake through a speckled brown alder bottom and sunny picnic site, into heavier forest.

The 6-km (3.6-mi) round trip trail to Anthony Lake (it begins to the right of the campsite) offers a shorter walk for the less ambitious or for people pushing strollers.

At the northern end, to the right of the long bridge, there is a beaver dam which has kept the marsh fairly dry. The trail leads through more dark forest out to Anthony Island, now linked with the main trail by a bridge. Mount Mahoney, on your right, overlooks this beautiful spot.

For shelter reservations call the Powell River Visitors Bureau at 485-4701.

Gallagher Hill Hike

This hike offers panoramic vistas of Powell Lake, Cranberry Lake, the Strait of Georgia and Westview. Look for wildflowers in season.

Access: From the Westview ferry terminal follow Marine (Hwy 101) north to the traffic light at Alberni Street. Turn right up Alberni to Manson Avenue, turn left and follow it to Cassiar Street, turn right on Cassiar, which runs into Yukon, and follow Yukon to Haslam Street. Turn right on Haslam and continue to the first junction and take the left branch, Inland Lake Road. Approximately 100 m (330 ft) up the Inland Lake Road, park where you see the trailhead leading off to the left.

Hiking Time/Distance: The approximately 1.8-km (1-mi) trail, a circle route, takes 1 3/4 to 2 hours to hike.

Description: Intermediate. This trail will get your heart pumping. From the trailhead, follow the fluorescent markers as the trail winds and twists through thick forest, takes switchbacks up steep hills, comes out on several sunny bluffs and descends again to the old road. Rock cairns on the upper bluffs point to the trail if you lose your way.

Forestry Museum Willingdon Beach Trail

This trail was once the rail bed of the Michigan and Puget Sound

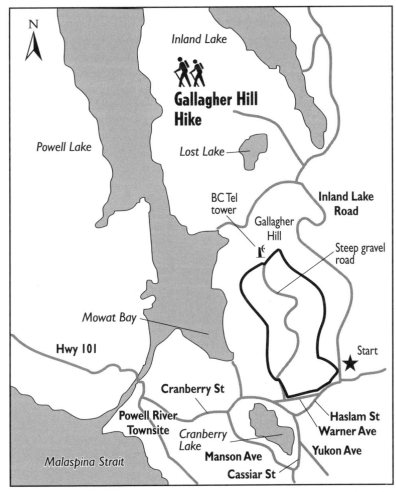

N

Inland Lake

Gallagher Hill Hike

Powell Lake

Lost Lake

BC Tel tower

Gallagher Hill

Inland Lake Road

Steep gravel road

Mowat Bay

Hwy 101

★ Start

Cranberry St

Powell River Townsite

Cranberry Lake

Manson Ave

Haslam St
Warner Ave

Yukon Ave

Malaspina Strait

Cassiar St

Logging company. Laid in 1910, it led from the log dumping wharf at the beach, then named Michigan Landing, along this trail, across the former golf course through the main intersection of the Townsite and down to Powell Lake across from today's Shinglemill Restaurant. (See map on page 159.)

Even before the logging, the entrance to the trail was steeped in history—the layers of clam shells bear evidence of the Sliammon Natives' 2,000-year occupancy. Be aware that BC law prohibits digging in these middens.

About 10 minutes in, the shore trail leads to the fringe of the forest where several virgin firs stand sentinel over a fascinating area of forest. Nurse stumps and logs are everywhere, young cedars form rainbows and four old cedars join to become one solid tree 1.2 m (4 ft) above the ground. Among this unusual vegetation are a number of logging relics brought from old camps around the district for display along the Forestry Museum trail.

Fishing off the pier and swimming are just two of the attractions of Willingdon Beach.

Access: From the Westview ferry terminal, go north along Marine (Hwy 101). Half a block past the traffic light at Alberni Street, park near the concession on the left. The trail starts at the yellow barrier by the creek.

Hiking Time/Distance: It takes only half an hour to cover the Museum trail to the far barrier and return and an additional 50 minutes to walk the round-trip trail that forks off the path.

Description: Primary to Intermediate. The main trail, the old rail bed trail, is excellent for the elderly and particularly great for a sunset stroll. The trail that dips down to the shore is more rugged. For the best view of the many old-growth trees, including some granddaddy maples, take the trail above the old rail bed on your way back.

Hazards: Off the main trail, the paths are often slippery and steep. Watch the tide if you decide to walk along the beach on your return trip. One or two spots are almost impassible at high tide.

HIKING ON TEXADA ISLAND

The Trekkers Hiking Group on the island meets every other Saturday at 10:00 a.m. to hike and clear one of the island's trails. Call 486-7100 if you would like to join them.

The Cornell Trail

This hike follows the route of the 1898 railway bed to the Cornell gold, silver and copper mine.

Most of the trail is primary, a cool shaded railbed padded with thick moss. The path by the creek takes you across the wooden bridge and comes

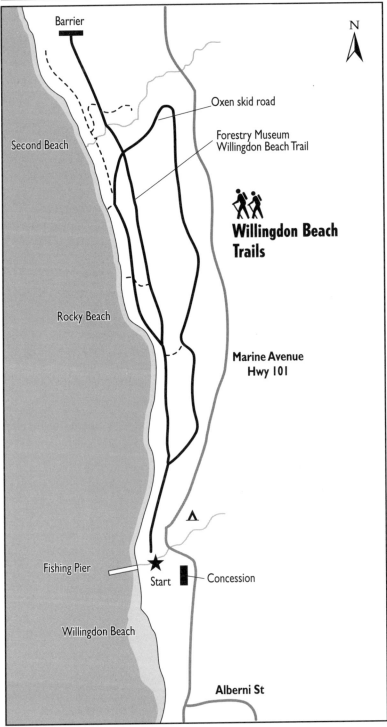

Barrier

Oxen skid road

Forestry Museum
Willingdon Beach Trail

Second Beach

**Willingdon Beach
Trails**

Rocky Beach

**Marine Avenue
Hwy 101**

Fishing Pier

Start

Concession

Willingdon Beach

Alberni St

N

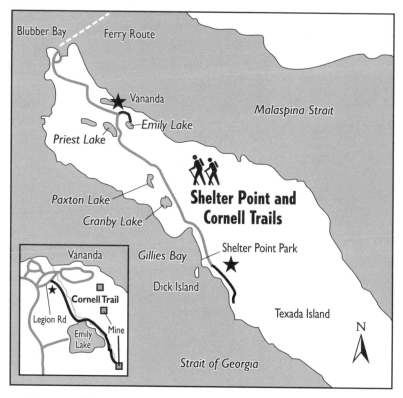

out into a small clearing by the lake. Dogwoods along the shore make the trail pretty in May. A rusted-out ore car, a few rotting logs shoring up the side of the mine workings and a boarded-up shaft are all that are left of the once-thriving mine.

Access: From the Westview ferry terminal, catch the late morning ferry to Blubber Bay and drive along the main road 9.5 km (5.7 mi) to the crossroads. Legion Road is just ahead; take it into the Legion Hall parking lot.

Hiking Time/Distance: It takes less than half an hour to reach the former Cornell mine site, a distance of 2.8 km (1.7 mi) one way, or 1 hour return.

Description: Intermediate. From the parking lot, walk down to the bottom of the hill and hook back on the right to the beginning of the trail. Ten minutes along the old railbed, alongside a churning creek and small falls, a path leads to the left. Follow this path until it reaches a road. Turn right and continue to the old mining area, ignoring the next road to the right.

Shelter Point Campsite and Trail

On the far side of the island, beautiful Shelter Point harbours a campground, a short, easy hiking trail and good ocean swimming.

Access: From the Blubber Bay ferry terminal, drive through Gillies Bay to the Shelter Point turnoff. The 40-minute round-trip hiking trail is well marked and leads from this corner. An excellent fringe of gnarled first-growth trees adds great interest to this trail. Look for the three-tined fir.

SWIMMING IN THE POWELL RIVER AREA

Mowat Bay: This is the area's most popular beach and is located on Powell Lake. For access, see the Mowat Bay to Powell Lake Shinglemill Hike in this section.

Willingdon Beach: This ocean beach is almost as popular as Mowat Bay. It offers picnic tables, washrooms and a playground for children. The beach is accessed from Highway 101 just north of the Westview business section.

Kinsman Park: A nice, sandy beach on Powell Lake near the Shinglemill. From Highway 101, turn right immediately past the Wildwood Bridge at the north end of town.

Inland Lake: If you are looking for something more remote, there are refreshing swimming spots around this lake. Combined with a hike, it is a wonderful way to spend an afternoon.

Shelter Point Regional Park (Texada Island): Good ocean swimming and picnicking. Warning: Don't try to walk out to the islet—strong currents have caused people to drown.

DIVING NEAR POWELL RIVER

The Wreck of the *Malahat*

The 33-m (109-ft) *Malahat* rests to the south of "The Hulks," World War II concrete transport carriers that form the breakwater for the mill log pond. The Hulks have been part of the historic scene since 1930, although the original boats have been replaced. An abundance of sea creatures can be found clinging to the undersides of these old boats.

Access: Follow Highway 101 north to the historic Powell River Townsite. Just past the viewpoint, turn left and take the MacMillan Bloedel road down to the first turnoff to the left. Park at the end of the road, past the last of the Hulks. There is a dive flag near the end of the rock breakwater.

Description: Primary to Intermediate. This area is teeming with marine life.

Depth: 12.2 to 27.4 m (40 to 90 ft).

Hazards: Fishermen and fishing lines.

WHERE TO STAY IN THE POWELL RIVER AREA

Adventure Bed and Breakfast. 7439 Nootka Street. Phone: 485-7097. Offers hiking, canoeing, sailing.

Beach Gardens Hotel. 7074 Westminster, Grief Point. Phone: 485-6267, toll-free:1-800-663-7070. Fax: 485-2343. Oceanfront, marina.

Beacon Bed and Breakfast. 3750 Marine, Westview. Phone: 485-5563. Oceanview suite, hot tub, Massage.

Coast Town Centre Hotel. 4660 Joyce Avenue, Westview. Phone: 485-3000. Fax: 485-3031. Worldwide Reservations toll-free 1-800-663-1144. Wheelchair accessible, hot tub, Convention Center.

E & E Bed and Breakfast. 6353 Oak Street, Historic Townsite. Phone: 483-3539. Garden setting, continental breakfast.

Eagle Mountain Bed and Breakfast. 7143 Ladner Street. Phone/fax: 485-2833. Garden setting, ocean view.

Hummingbird Bed and Breakfast. 7139 Ladner Street. Phone/fax: 485-5658. Panoramic ocean view, private suite.

Hyatt Motor Lodge. 6255 Marine Avenue, in the historic Townsite. Phone: 483-3113. Fax: 483-2121. Toll-free 1-800-669-3319.

The Inn at Westview. 7050 Alberni, Westview. Phone: 485-6281. Fax: 485-2622

Marine Inn. 4429 Marine, Westview. Phone: 485-4242.

Marland Motel. 7156 Thunder Bay, Grief Point. Phone: 485-4435. Fax: 485-0175

Old Courthouse Inn. 6243 Walnut Street, Powell River. Phone: 483-4000 or 1-877-473-4777. Email: oldcourt@telus.net.

Seaside Villa Motel & RV Park. 7274 Hwy 101, Grief Point. Phone: 485-2911. Call toll-free: 1-877-485-2911. Fax: 485-6268.

Westview Centre Motel. 4534 Marine Avenue, Westview. Phone: 485-4023. Call Toll Free: 1-877-485-4023. Fax: 485-7736. Ocean view.

Texada Shores. 2790 Sanderson Road, Gillies Bay, Texada Island. Phone: 486-7388. Highbank waterfront, hearty breakfast.

DINING OUT IN THE POWELL RIVER AREA

$ means 2 people can eat, have a bottle of wine (if licensed) and get out for under $30 or so. $$ is $40–$50 and $$$ is over $50.

Coast Hotel Garden Court, 4660 Joyce, 485-3000. Known for its seafood. $$$

Chiang Mai Thai Restaurant, 4463 Marine, 485-0883. $

Deli Truce European Restaurant, 4480 Willingdon, 485-9224. $$

Grenada Restaurant & Pizza, 6249 Marine. Historic Townsite. 483-3333. Known for its steak and seafood. $$$

Gourmet Canton, 7-7030 Glacier, 485-2885. Try the curried prawn or mixed meat hot plate. $$

Jitterbug Cafe, 4643 Marine Avenue, 485-7797. Casual dining with steak & seafood, ocean view. $$$

Kane's Sports Bar & Bistro, 4-7030 Alberni Street, 485-7666. Reasonable steak dinners. $

New Moon Palace, 4801 Joyce, 485-4632. Chinese specialties. $$

Oriental, 4432 Marine, 485-9533. Overlooks the ocean. Heaping plates of Chinese Food. $$

Shinglemill Restaurant, 6233 Powell Place, 483-2001. Great old-fashioned, mouth-watering prime rib and Yorkshire pudding. $$$

Snickers, 4591 Marine. Phone: 485-8441. Greek, Italian and French cuisine. Waterfront view. $$

Westview Pizza & Spaghetti, 4553 Marine, 485-6162 or 485-9731. The best pizza in town. $$$

Whooters' Restaurant, 4680 Marine Avenue, 485-0970. Fine dining, seafood and other specialties. $$$

Besides the establishments listed above, there are many other fast-food and cafe-type eateries in the Powell River area.

POWELL RIVER TO LUND

Wildwood to Lund: A Trip to the End of the Road

Sliammon Village is the oldest settlement on this part of the coast. Captain George Vancouver marked it on the map of his historic 1791 voyage, and it probably goes back centuries before that. Carbon dating has confirmed that the Coast Salish Sliammon, a peaceful fishing people, have lived in the area for at least 2,000 years.

Sliammon villagers enjoy an old-fashioned totem-raising.

When the white man began visiting the shores of the area, trapping, prospecting and felling the virgin forests, Tom Timothy was the hereditary chief of the Sliammon First Nation. He led his band for seventy years until, in 1953, he turned over the Native government to Charlie Peters, the first elected chief.

The Natives eagerly embraced the game of soccer, producing many renowned players, and a park on the east side of the highway was built expressly for soccer. The totem pole outside the park was carved by Jackie Timothy, Tom Timothy's great-nephew.

The Sliammon Salmon Hatchery just before the bridge over Sliammon Creek, is open to the public when the workers are on the premises. This is a wonderful place to see salmon enhancement at work. Call ahead to reserve a tour; 483-4111. From the 2nd to 3rd week of March the coho, chinook, and chum fingerlings are emerging from their eggs and will incubate until the end of May. They feed eight times a day, seven days a week. From September to November, the salmon return to the creek and the eggs are collected. The hatchery produces 1–1.5 million fish annually.

For a flavour of Sliammon culture, try a Coast Salish Tour. Their headquarters is located at Lund Hotel from June 1 to September 30. Phone: 483-4505 for information; toll-free 1-800-345-1112 to book tours. Visit their website at www.ayjoomixw.com. Kayak and canoe tours are offered; a 30-foot dugout canoe glides into Desolation Sound or over to Harwood Island. Or take an interpretive hike or walk and discover medicinal plants and other natural resources used in basket weaving.

Back on the highway, you will soon pass Scuttle Bay. Across the highway is the turnoff to Wilde Road, which once led to Wilde's Mink Farm. It is now the access to Sliammon Lake and the Appleton Canyon hike.

The Klahanie and Southview areas boast some of the loveliest seashores in the district, with the appeal of spectacular sunsets, sandy beaches and a view of nearby Harwood Island.

Lacy trees frame the panorama seen from this stretch of highway. Beyond Southview, Gifford and Atrevida Roads on your left and Craig Road on your right, where local residents got together to build a handsome park, is the Old Mine Road. An iron mine was worked here sometime after 1916, with the ore trucked to Lund to be sent

In 1947 the MV Gulfstream ran up on Dinner Rock, taking five lives.

out by boat. The tunnel still runs under the highway.

The fastest oyster-shucker on the coast of BC grew up in the Southview area. Mary (Powell) Masales, whose father surveyed the Townsite before the advent of the mill, could shuck approximately 700 oysters an hour!

Less than .5 km (.3 mi) from the Old Mine Road is a road that signs identify as both the Browne Creek and the Dinner Rock Road. This is your access to that part of the Sunshine Coast Trail that leads to the Dinner Rock campsite. However, it is not the closest road to the campsite. That's the *next* road, almost 2 km (1.2 mi) on, past the coniferous forest planted by MacMillan Bloedel in 1992, to be harvested in 60 years or so. This road is *also* called Dinner Rock Road and appears as such on maps.

The Dinner Rock Trail is a section of the Greenways Project, a cycling trail which connects to the trail leading from the Dinner Rock Road in the other direction. It features some interesting carvings. Jackie Timothy, inspired by the setting, sculpted a killer whale in a stump here. His brother Alvin roughed out an eagle (thunderbird) in a log. The carvings were admired by the Forest Service Recreation people, giving them the idea of adding the totem pole and carvings to the Inland Lake trail, a project carried out in 1995.

If you are hiking the circle route trail to the coral and green rock slab beaches of the Dinner Rock Campsite, drive partway down and park your car at the pull-off. Take the trail to your right (facing the water) as the loose rock and steepness of the road to the site makes walking awkward. It's easier to complete the circle hike by walking up the road. If you're carting in camping supplies, a truck or four-wheeler will serve you best.

About 1.5 km (.9 mi) farther along the highway is Malaspina Road, which winds down to Okeover Arm, a quiet arm of the ocean on the east side of Malaspina Peninsula, where, past the restaurant at the foot of the hill, there is a small government campground with 5 sites. The Laughing Oyster Restaurant is open year-round (closed Monday and Tuesday in winter) offering a varied menu with seafood specialties. The oysters in the area are on a private lease, please be considerate. Try the delicious oysters in the restaurant instead.

The historic Lund Hotel
marks the end (or beginning) of 24,000-km Highway 101.

*The historic Lund waterwheel can be seen
beyond the craft shop.*

If you are looking for something in this area that is less rustic than the campsite, either Cedar Lodge Bed and Breakfast or Desolation Sound Resort just off Malaspina Road will fill the bill. A government wharf and boat ramp offer overnight moorage and allow you to launch your own boat. Or you can rent a boat from Y-Knot Boat Rentals on the corner of Malaspina and Highway 101 and cruise Desolation Sound–Prideau Haven, Grace Harbour and Tenedos Bay.

You are now only 3 km (1.8 mi) away from the end or as the Lund residents say, the beginning of Highway 101, about 30 km (18 mi) northwest of Powell River. Lund and London, England lie on approximately the same latitude, 50 degrees north.

Although a magazine once falsely reported that Lund was established in 1970 by American draft dodgers and others pursuing an alternate lifestyle, Lund was actually founded in 1889 by the Thulin brothers, Fred and Carl (Charles). Little did they know at the time that the logging road they would build would become the beginning of a highway that would stretch 24,000 km (14,400 mi) to Puerto Monte, Chile, in South America.

Drive down into the fishing village and park across from the Lund

Hotel and walk down to the government wharf. Below you, fluorescent orange and purple starfish are visible on the harbour bottom, obscured only by dense schools of minnows gliding through the clear Pacific water. Beyond, to the right, is a charming fishing centre called Finn Bay, and beyond the harbour limits, the southern end of the Copeland Islands, better known locally as the Ragged Islands. Savary Island is on your right and Hernando centre left. Far across the Strait of Georgia is the massive snow-covered spine of Vancouver Island's central mountain range. The harbour is full of character boats of all kinds, and is framed by boardwalks and beach-hugging buildings that recall an earlier era of coastal life. Lund's centrepiece is the historic "Malaspina Hotel." In 1999, the Sliammon First Nations and local entrepreneur Dave Formosa purchased and renovated the hotel and renamed it the Lund Resort. Its restaurant and pub offer refreshment of any kind plus a view to be enjoyed in all weathers, all year round. A general store in the same building is also licensed to sell liquor, wine and beer.

Behind the hotel, you might be lucky enough to find well-known native carver, Jackie Timothy, and an appealing craft gallery.

The trail leading around the boat basin past the large water wheel, takes you out to seasonal eating spots that almost rival Nancy's Bakery on the wharf. To the left of this bakery and down the ramp, is the Lund Water Taxi.

Lund is very special for its blend of natural beauty and historic character, making it the perfect place to conclude—or begin anew—your exploration of the Sunshine Coast and its wonders.

Lund—Founded on a Rumour

Lund, the beginning or end of a 24,000-km (14,400-mi) highway, owes its existence to a rumour heard in Sweden in the nineteenth century:

"Poppa" Fred Thulin and his brother founded Lund in 1889.

Canadians don't have to work in the rain. Fred Thulin, age 16, believed it and came out to meet his brother Charlie on Redonda Island in Pendrell Sound in March 1889. The brothers handlogged in the area until December—which gave them ample time to curse this particular rumour—then came down to a little bay on the Malaspina Peninsula, where they built a log wharf that became the cornerstone of the town of Lund. Fred said they chose the Swedish town-name "Lund" because it was easy to remember and easy to spell. In Swedish, it means "forest grove."

After building the wharf, they piped fresh water to supply the steamers, cleared land and cut cordwood to sell to the tugs, fished at night for dogfish livers to make oil that sold for 25 cents a gallon, opened a post office in 1892 for which they made their own mail bags, built a store, and in 1894, opened the first licensed hotel north of

Vancouver, and built an open-air pavilion. In 1895, they built a new hotel containing the post office and store and even a "jail" in the basement for the rowdies.

In 1904, the Thulin Brothers expanded their operations across the Strait of Georgia to Vancouver Island, erecting the first building in what would become Campbell River. The Thulin partnership was dissolved in 1927, and Charlie Thulin took over the task of nurturing Campbell River into a thriving city while Fred, whose friends called him "Poppa," remained in Lund until his death in 1935 at the age of 62.

We can thank the Thulin brothers for beginning two important settlements on the coast—all because they'd heard Canadians didn't work in the rain!

Looking down on "Ayhus" (Savary Island), named for the legendary double-headed serpent of Sliammon myth.

Savary Island

"Savary's Isle" was named by Captain George Vancouver in 1792, possibly after Admiral Savary of the French Navy who was serving in the Caribbean when Vancouver passed through there.

This "tropic isle" was called *Ayhus* by the Sliammon, after a two-headed serpent who lived in a cave where the island is today. One day the monster slithered out and went on an eating binge, devouring everything in sight: seals and salmon, even people it tipped out of canoes, topped off with a killer whale or two. The Great Transformer was so displeased with this display of greed that he turned the serpent into an island.

Ayhus proved to be a more attractive island than monster, for not even Captain George Vancouver, whose bleak descriptions of many West Coast features seemed to suggest they were merely obstacles between him and the

Northwest Passage, could find anything miserable to say about the Island.

It actually has a desert climate, and is oriented east–west rather than north–south like most of the rocky islands of British Columbia.

Deep depressions in the meadow suggest that the Sliammon band lived in underground *kekuli*, perhaps as a protection from the fierce Haida who raided the clam beds, carried off women and children and beheaded those men they had no further use for. They made slaves of their captives, taking some men to do their paddling, but cutting their ankle tendons first.

This giant arbutus tree is claimed to be the largest in the world.

The first white man on the island, John Green, came in 1886 at the age of 69. He was retiring from a life of farming on Vancouver Island and running a trading boat, the *Wanderer*, up and down the coast. He set up his trading post near the east end, officially called Mace Point but known locally as Green Point. He built two houses, storage and animal outbuildings, and raised sheep, pigs and chickens. When he became too old to handle it all himself he took in a partner, Tom Taylor, and invested his money in more island land. Before the papers could be signed on the last piece of land he'd applied for in 1893, he and his partner were robbed and murdered. Hugh Lynn was hanged for the murder. Rumours of Green's fortune lured treasure hunters to the area, but if they found anything, they told no one.

Louis Anderson was Savary's next pioneer; then came the Savary Island Syndicate, who divided much of the island into 15-m (50-ft) lots, city-style.

Over the years, the white sands of Savary have brought excursionists in droves. The Union Steamships *Lady Cecilia* and *Lady Cynthia* from 1933 to 1940 brought an average of 400 passengers per trip—and this was during the Depression! Of course Depression prices were in effect; for $2.00, one could cruise for 160 miles. By the 1950s, air service and water taxis replaced the boat trips. The next wave of settlers in the seventies were not readily welcomed in an area that still considered the 1926 Royal Savary Hotel people "newcomers."

Today, new development on the island is limited to 4-hectare (10-acre) lots. Islanders enjoy their own newspaper, church and airport. Since

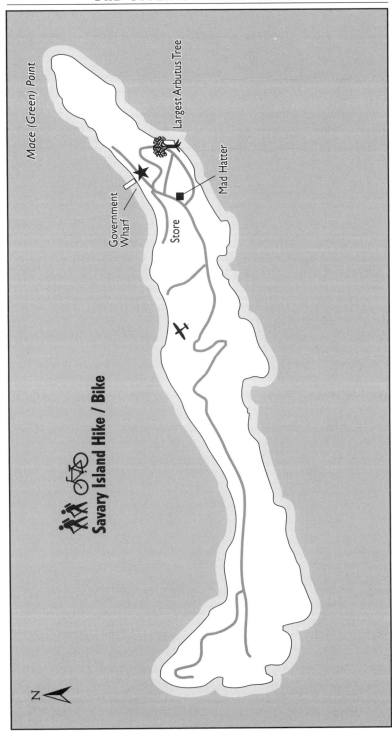

Mace (Green) Point

Largest Arbutus Tree

Mad Hatter

Government Wharf

Store

Savary Island Hike / Bike

N

stringent fire and health laws brought about the demise of the Royal Savary Hotel in 1983, a much-needed meeting place, the Mad Hatter Restaurant, opened in 1984.

The largest arbutus tree in the world still grows on the island's south side. It is located on private property; please visit only between 10 am – 4 pm.

SWIMMING NORTH OF POWELL RIVER

Gibsons Beach: This municipal ocean beach is located adjacent to Highway 101 between Wildwood and Lund.

Savary Island: This island is surrounded by white sand beaches and only a boat ride away from Lund. See the charter boat listings in the appendix to reach the water taxi.

HIKING TRAILS IN THE LUND AREA

Marathon, Rieveley's Pond and Appleton Trail Systems

These three trails all have something to offer: Giant old-growth Douglas firs on the valley floor give the Appleton Canyon special appeal; Rieveley's Pond is a haven for birds; Marathon's views are breathtaking. All three trails have picnic tables and outhouses.

Access: Follow Highway 101 north past the village of Sliammon to Southview Road. About 4.5 km (2.7 mi) in on Southview, a sign marks the trailhead. Take the "Gentle David" turn for an outstanding view of the Strait of Georgia. Follow along again until you reach another viewpoint, "Gibraltar." Marathon ends here.

Retrace your steps or continue. Another half hour's hiking will take you to Rieveley's Pond, and from there, a further hour's hike will bring you to Appleton Creek Recreation Site. A 2.2-km (1.3-mi) extension begins close to the Homestead Recreation Site, following the creek.

Appleton Creek alone may be accessed by travelling 6 km (3.6 mi) up Wilde Road. This is one of those hikes which you might like to do with a friend, leaving a vehicle at each end.

Dinner Rock Hiking and Biking Trail

A variety of vegetation and topography makes this switchback trail a hiker's delight. Fern-fringed forest trails lead out to moss-covered sunny bluffs and then through a pine forest to ocean lookouts. White soapberry bushes and the red hips of the Nootka rose among the pines and arbutus brighten even the greyest winter day. Savary is the first island you see from the trail. It is often described as a snake, with the "head" facing the mainland. (See map on page 174.)

Access: From the Westview Wharf area, travel 25 minutes north on

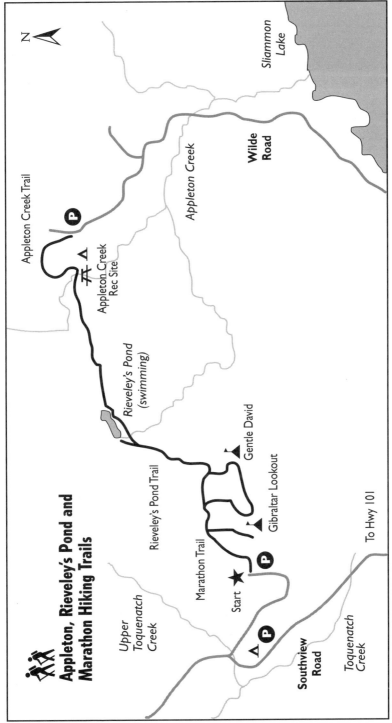

Appleton, Rieveley's Pond and Marathon Hiking Trails

Highway 101 to the Dinner Rock Campsite sign, 2 km (1.2 mi) past the Browne Creek–Dinner Rock sign. From October to May, the campsite road is closed to vehicles. Walk down the upper part of this road and turn right at the Powell River Greenways trail sign. Bicycles are welcome but motorized "dirt bikes" are not.

Travelling farther over the bluffs, up by the picnic tables and through the trail, you come out at another viewpoint overlooking Dinner Rock on the left, Savary Island centre, and Hernando Island on the far right. Bald eagles soar above the coral (below) and green-coloured rock (far right).

Dinner Rock was the scene of a marine disaster on October 11, 1947 when the MV *Gulfstream* ran up on the rock. Five people were drowned but only four bodies were recovered. The cross on the rock is in memory of the

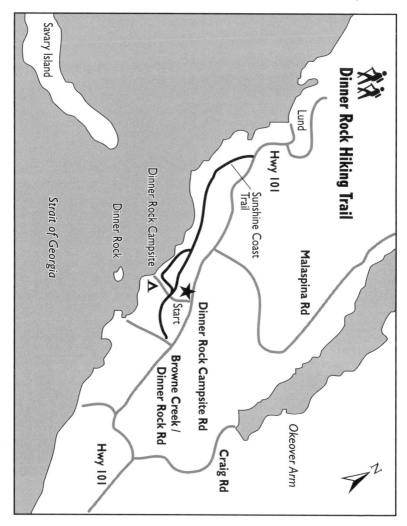

little girl who was never found.

Hiking Time/Distance: The 1.7-km (1-mi) trail to the campsite takes 1 hour or less. Double that if you plan to return the same way. The other option is to walk up the campsite road at the beginning of the trail, which is steep but shorter, only 20 minutes slow walking.

Description: Primary to Intermediate. The first part of this well-developed trail covers part of the 180-km (108-mi) Sunshine Coast Trail that connects Saltery Bay and Sarah Point. Across the Forest Service road from the trailhead sign, you will notice another link to this trail. (Keep on this trail if you wish to explore the Sunshine Coast Trail further.) Turn left at the sign to Dinner Rock to bring you to the beach.

BIKING IN THE LUND AREA

Bunster Hills Bike Loop

This "killer" 750-m (2,475-ft) climb rewards the rider with super views of Okeover Inlet and and the Strait of Georgia. (See map on page 176.)

Access: Take Highway 101 north to Wilde Road, approx. 13 km (8 mi) north from the Westview ferry terminal at Powell River. Turn right on Wilde and park.

Riding time/Distance: 4 to 5 hours, 34 km (20.4 mi).

Description: The route is marked counterclockwise with either a white biking symbol or a double band of orange paint.

Follow Wilde Road for 2 km (1.2 mi) where the road becomes Theodosia Forest Service Road and begin the 12-km (7.2-mi) climb. About halfway up the climb, you will pass the Appleton Creek Trail. Stay on the main road. After a 6-km (3.6-mi) descent, turn left at the intersection. Follow this road for approx. 3 km (1.8 mi) to a fork, Southview Road. Turn left, follow Southview for 3 km (1.8 mi) back to the highway. Turn left to return to the start of the loop.

The Sunshine Coast is a haven for mountain bikers.

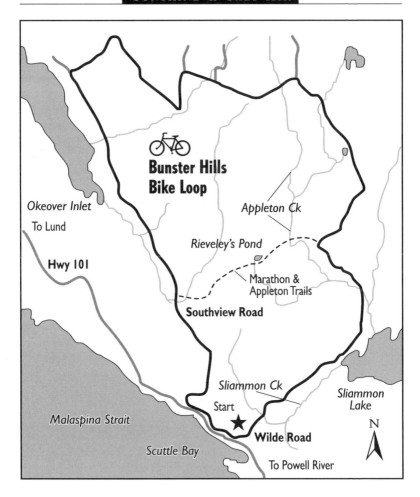

**Bunster Hills
Bike Loop**

Okeover Inlet

To Lund

Hwy 101

Appleton Ck

Rieveley's Pond

Marathon &
Appleton Trails

Southview Road

Sliammon Ck

Sliammon
Lake

Start

Malaspina Strait

Wilde Road

Scuttle Bay

To Powell River

N

DIVES NORTH OF POWELL RIVER

Adventurer Shore Dive

Colourful creatures cling to several wrecks in this area. Although the 10-m (33-ft) *Adventurer* is just a skeleton now, there is the 15-m (50-ft) tug nearer shore, a rowboat, and a recently sunk 9-m (30-ft) cabin cruiser called *Skookum*.

Access: Take Highway 101 to Lund and turn right on to Finn Bay Road, just past the garage. Follow almost to the end of the road and park. Find the trail marked with a dive flag in the tree. At the end of this path, look southwest and line up the dive flags. Over the ledge to the left is an old tugboat. The *Adventurer* is almost straight out from this craft.

Description: Wall dive. Beginner to Advanced depending on how adventurous you get. The visibility here is great below the plankton.

Depth: 15.2 m (50 ft).

Hazards: Don't leave home without your dive flag as this area abounds with boaters.

Okeover Caves Boat Dive

There are three caves at different levels: 9.1 m (30 ft), 18.3 m (60 ft) and 27.4 m (90 ft). Over the black cliff wall, anemones form a living tapestry.

Access: Travel north on Highway 101 to Malaspina Road. Turn right and go down into the arm where you may launch your boat to the right of the government dock. The caves are almost directly across the arm on a sheer wall marked with a dive flag.

Description: Advanced boat dive. The lowest cave looks more like a cavern with a pile of rubble in front. Hydroids like ferns and sparklers abound, and nudibranchs flow with the current.

Depth: 30.5 m (100 ft).

Hazards: This dive must be done only with proper training and equipment.

A rockfish stares down an underwater cameraman.
Small but feisty, these fish may live as long as 80 years.

The Iron Mines Boat Dive

You never know what you will run into in these crystal clear waters; there is always something new. Among the amazingly various and abundant marine life are the giant cloud sponge, the tube sponge and hanging gardens of colourful anemones.

Access: Take Highway 101 north to Lund. Launch your boat here and head south a short distance to the waterfall on the second point of land.

Description: Boat dive. Advanced, but a newer diver with good buoyancy control might attempt it with caution. This dive is reputed to be the best on the BC coast!

Depth: Watch your gauge as it drops off to 122 m (400 ft) here.

Hazards: Currents, the depth and overhead boat traffic present a number of dangers.

For Further Consideration:

The Union Steamships began regular service on the Sunshine Coast around 100 years ago. Before that there were many popular moorages along the coast. Bottle divers and underwater archaeologists know and cherish these spots. If you get friendly with one, you may get some inside information.

WHERE TO STAY IN LUND

Dinner Rock Forest Service Campground. Dinner Rock Road. Rustic.

North of Lund,
Desolation Sound is a boater's paradise.

Blue Heron Tourist Suite. 4111 Lund Hwy. Phone: 483-7907. Spacious ocean-front one bedroom suite with panoramic view.

Cedar Lodge Bed and Breakfast. 9825 Malaspina Road. Phone/Fax: 483-4414. European-style in serene setting.

Desolation Sound Resort. 2694 Dawson Road. Phone: 483-3592. Fax: 483-7942. Deluxe units overlooking Okeover Arm, kitchens.

Hikers Haven B&B, Gifford Road (ten minutes south of Lund). Phone: 483-4665. Fax 483-2350. Access to the Sunshine Coast Trail at the back door.

Lund Hotel. 1436 Lund Highway, 414-0474. Enjoy the ambiance of this newly-renovated heritage hotel. Marina and store..

Lund RV Park & Campground. Off Hwy. 101. Phone: 483-4463. Take Larson Road next to school.

Savary Island Lodge B&B. Phone: 483-9481. Updated 1930s log cabin on sunny Savary Island.

The Oyster Shell Beach House. 3879 Hwy 101. Phone: 414-0231. Fax: 483-4986. One bedroom suite near great shellfish beach.

Y Knot Charters & Campground. D'angio Road. Okeover Arm, turn right at Malaspina Road. Phone: 483-3243. View of inlet, limited facilities.

DINING OUT IN THE LUND AREA

As prices change with the economy we have used $ signs to indicate relative prices.

$ means 2 people can eat, have a bottle of wine (if licensed) and get out for under $30 or so. $$ is $40–$50 and $$$ is over $50.

Lund Hotel Restaurant. 1436 Lund Hwy. Phone: 414-0474 Fabulous harbour and bay view. $$$

Laughing Oyster Restaurant, 10052 Malaspina Road, 483-9775. Overlooking a quiet arm of the ocean. Excellent cuisine, seafood specialties. $$$

4

FOUR-WHEELING ON THE SUNSHINE COAST

By Keith Thirkell & David Lee

F ew visitors to the Sunshine Coast are aware that hundreds of miles of back roads offer a quite different recreational experience from that of the settled areas. Settlement has naturally hugged the shoreline, so the main highway follows the relatively mild ups and downs of a narrow strip of coast. But look over your shoulder and you'll be assaulted by great walls of green hillsides that conceal the coast's real back country.

Since much of the territory is laced with logging roads, it offers owners of off-road vehicles a matchless opportunity to splash some mud on their fenders and see some truly spectacular country.

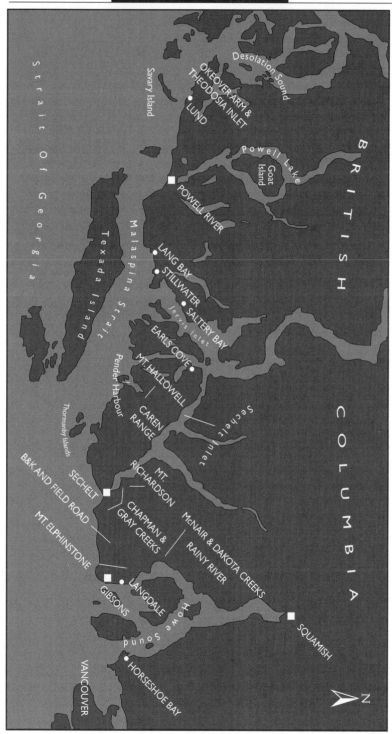

A few words of advice and caution are in order:

• You are in logging country. Most of the 4x4 roads are here because of the logging industry so watch out! Always travel back roads with your headlights on. Weekends are the best time to venture out because loggers generally aren't on the job.

• Radios and scanners are fun but can also be lifesavers. Citizen's band radios are good for communicating with other off-roaders, and on weekdays, police scanners allow you to pick up VHF radio logging traffic to avoid unwelcome faceoffs with logging trucks.

• It's a good idea to inform someone of roughly where you plan to go and how long you expect to be there. Travelling in groups is also a good idea.

• Carry a little emergency equipment: matches, warm clothes, spare food, spare tire, jack, a few

A very common sight in the summer. Black bears enjoy old logging roads too.

tools, spare water for the radiator, maps, and radios or scanners if you're travelling logging roads on weekdays.

• You're on your own. This section is simply a guide: the information provided is accurate within reason, but conditions in the back country change constantly, roads may be washed out, and users of this information do so at their own risk.

Hold on a minute, what *is* a 4x4?

True four-wheeling is not for the average Subaru sedan. Road conditions vary immensely. Some are suitable for low-ground clearance "All Wheel Drive" cars and vans, but it's a huge overstatement to describe a lot of 4x4 routes as "roads." In Mark Bostwick's popular guidebook, *The Four-Wheeler's Companion to Southwestern BC* (Harbour Publishing, 3rd edition 1995), he rates back roads according to class of difficulty: from one to ten:

1 Very easy
2 Easy
3 Moderate
4 Moderately difficult
5 Difficult
6 Difficult and perhaps dangerous to the vehicle
7 Very difficult and dangerous
8 Extremely difficult and dangerous
9 Expeditionary driving
10 The impossible (until someone does it!)

Bostwick's book supplies more detailed definitions of each class. In general, classes 1 to 3 are suitable for 4x4 cars and vans with limited ground clearance. But anything in the Class 4 range and up warrants a real 4x4 with good ground clearance and tires with serious traction. Routes above Class 6 are for serious monster trucks only: gumbo mudder tires, 5 feet off the ground and all the gizmos like roll bars and winches. Class 10 routes are a challenge to even the best armored personnel carrier!

So now you're ready to go four-wheelin'!

What follows is a partial list of some of the better known and more interesting Sunshine Coast back roads. Some routes are described in more detail than others, but most just give a rough definition of location and class rating. The rest is up to you and your spirit of adventure. Have fun.

Maps

The best sources for maps on the Sunshine Coast are the Government Agent in Teredo Square in Sechelt, and the Ministry of Forests on Field Road in Wilson Creek. Ask them for any recreation maps for the region. In Powell River, the Government Agent on Alberni Street is the best source.

AREA ONE: HOWE SOUND

These routes start at Port Mellon and work back toward Gibsons.

Rainy River

Good views of Panther Peak on the middle section and the Tetrahedron farther up are highlights, but the going gets tough. Accessible from the

*Dakota Creek offers a range
of challenges and rewards for the four-wheeler.*

4

Howe Sound Pulp & Paper mill at Port Mellon. The gate at the mill may be closed, but a polite request at the gatehouse should get you through. The road follows the crystal clear Rainy River high into the mountains behind the mill, quickly becoming a Class 6 route. For the avid bushwhacker, hiking into the newly established Tetrahedron Provincial Park is a real possibility from this route. Class 5–6.

McNair Creek

10 km (6 mi) from the Langdale ferry terminal, just before you enter the little town of Port Mellon—known all along the Sunshine Coast as "Dogpatch"—you cross a bridge. Take the first left past the bridge and snake your way past the gravel pit. Don't get distracted by all the side roads; stay on the main road up the hill as far as you can go.

The road gets ugly fast, but persistence will pay off. You'll go past huge cliffs beset by spring rockslides, about 6 km (3.6 mi) up a gorgeous little valley that's full of

Beautiful, clean waterfalls where water bottles and radiators can be topped up in the McNair Valley.

black bears, so in the fall watch out for hunters. At the end of the road a trail leads through a magnificent stand of old growth mountain hemlock trees to a beautiful little waterfall and a cabin at McNair Lake. The tranquility of that cabin is well worth the hard drive up. Class 6–7.

Dakota Creek

If you stay on this road it will eventually take you to the Tetrahedron and/or Sechelt. This is mainline logging country and the road is wide and well used. You can reach it at the beginning of an S-curve on the uphill side of the Sunshine Coast Highway about 7.5 km (4.5 mi) from the Langdale ferry terminal. It veers sharply to the left, then climbs straight up for miles. At the top, 4–5 km (2.4–3 mi) from the pavement, there's a great view of Port Mellon and Howe Sound. Branches off this mainline are too numerous to list but well worth a few days' exploration. Class 2–3.

East Face of Mt. Elphinstone

If you can find this road you deserve all the fun that it offers the die-hard four-wheeler with a good truck. About 2.5 km (1.5 mi) from the Langdale ferry terminal you'll see an overgrown road veering off to the left. It gets grizzly quick. Cross ditches big enough to swallow a D-8 cat await the unsuspecting. Once past these, you take switchback after switchback straight up. Eventually you're literally hugging the face of Mt. Elphinstone with a view that *almost* makes it worthwhile. I fully expect someone to ride a landslide down this road someday. No one I know has braved the last section of narrow ledge across loose rubble to tell me what's over the top. Class 6–8.

AREA TWO: ROBERTS CREEK

B&K Mainline

This is the main industrial road heading up the mountain from Roberts Creek and over the west shoulder of Mt. Elphinstone. Accessible about 10 km (6 mi) north of Sunnycrest Mall in Gibsons on the Sunshine Coast Highway, where a sign identifies the Roberts Creek Forest Service Road. At the top (about 9 km/5.4 mi from the highway) a sharp S-turn connects the road with the Dakota Mainline, mentioned earlier (Dakota Creek). Offshoots from the B&K connect with Wilson Creek, and indirectly with Sechelt. Class 3.

Mid-Elphinstone, Paisley Lookout

About halfway (4.5 km/2.7 mi) up the B&K Mainline a little-used road heads off to the right. You're immediately confronted with "Squamish culverts," as I call them, better known as "cross ditches" and/or "water bars." But after a mile or two on this road an opening gives an expansive view over outer Howe Sound, directly in line with the Paisleys, a tranquil little chain of pretty green islands. Class 4.

West Face of Mt. Elphinstone

A beautiful lookout off the B&K, about 5 km (3 mi) from the highway, can be found by veering sharply to the right on a raunchy old goat track that leads almost straight up the west face of Elphinstone. Crevices and sinkholes make this an especially challenging route, better undertaken with an aggressive motocross bike. But the view from the top, usually approached by foot after abandoning any attempts to make it up under motor power, is stunning. The Strait of Georgia spreads out at your feet. Great sunsets. Class 8 (there are rumours that this road has been improved, but by the time you read this, the raincoast being what it is, conditions on this climb could very well have degenerated to normal).

Field Road

At the Wilson Creek IGA, turn up Field Road and drive until the pavement ends, then turn right and keep going. Miles of snaking gravel await. There are connections to Chapman Creek Road and the Dakota mainline. Class 3.

*The Chapman Plateau offers
unlimited rambling for the backcountry adventurer.*

AREA THREE: SECHELT

Upper Chapman Valley

More wonderful views, this time of Sechelt and the Trail Islands. From the main stoplight in Sechelt, head east along Wharf Road and three blocks later turn right onto Porpoise Bay Road. Follow the signs to the Sunshine Coast Regional District dump, where the pavement ends. Keep going straight and turn right at the T-junction. This road seems to go forever, past beautiful Chapman Creek, where excursions on foot will reveal great swimming holes in summer and who knows, maybe the odd fish. But please be careful: this is the water supply for most of the area. The upper reaches of this road are unforgiving and change monthly, but there's great four-wheeling to be found. The avid bushwhacker will find himself on the doorstep of the new Tetrahedron Provincial Park. Class 3–4.

Gray Creek

This infamous road takes the enthusiastic hiker to the heart of the Tetrahedron. From the main stoplight in Sechelt, head east along Wharf Road and three blocks later turn right onto Porpoise Bay Road. Pass the Porpoise Bay Provincial Park, and about 9 km (5.4 mi) from Sechelt you'll see on the left the Jackson Dry Land Sort and on the right a road that is variously called the Gray Creek Reservoir Road, the Jackson Brothers mainline or the

*The long climb up Mt. Richardson
is full of scenic rewards.*

Tetrahedron mainline. Whatever it's called, it gets there by going—where else?—straight up. Eventually—about 13 km (7.8 mi) from the pavement—you'll reach the Tetrahedron Provincial Park parking lot. The trails await, and four beautiful cabins are at your disposal, but you'll have to walk a few miles to find them. Class 3–4.

Mt. Richardson

From the main stoplight in Sechelt, head east along Wharf Road and three blocks later turn right onto Porpoise Bay Road. Pass the Porpoise Bay Provincial Park, and about 9 km (5.4 mi) from Sechelt you'll see on the left the Jackson Dry Land Sort and on the right, as described in the Gray Creek route, the Gray Creek Reservoir Road. Set your odometer at 0, turn up this road and at 1.2 km (.7 mi) take the left fork. At 14.2 km (8.5 mi) take the left fork going up, following an old stream bed part of the way until at 15.5 km (9.3 mi) there's a forest service sign for the Mt. Richardson Recreation Site, and a fork in the road. The left fork takes you a few hundred yards to Richardson Lake, where there's a small campsite and lots of trout. The right fork curves up onto Mt. Richardson's northwest brow, for an absolutely breathtaking view of the Sechelt Inlet area, including the Skookumchuck Narrows, the Caren Range, and Mount Tzoonie.

AREA FOUR: SECHELT PENINSULA

Carlson and Crowston lakes

If back country fishing's your bag, there are a couple of little lakes behind Halfmoon Bay where I hear trout beg to be caught. In the curve just south of Trout Lake on the Sunshine Coast Highway, about 10 km (6 mi) north of the main stoplight in Sechelt, a dirt road switches back up off the pavement; follow this for about 5 ugly kilometres (3 mi). If you keep to the right at all forks you'll wind up at Crowston Lake. Around 6 km (3.6 mi), just off the Caren mainline logging road, a road to the right will eventually take you to Carlson Lake. A great place to bring a canoe, a frying pan and lots of patience. Class 3–5.

Caren Mainline

At the bottom of the Halfmoon Bay hill on the Sunshine Coast Highway about 13 km (7.8 mi) north of the main stoplight in Sechelt, a paved road leads off to the right. Follow this past the Wildlife Rehabilitation Centre. Keep going until you hit gravel. At about 13 km (7.8 mi) from the highway you can go any one of three ways, each of which takes you into the heart of Canada's oldest known forest: the Caren Range, now famous as the place where Canada's first active marbled murrelet nest was found. Some of these trees—what's left of them—are at least 2,000 years old. The attractions of several little lakes offer soothing reprieves from whatever mun-

Canada's oldest known trees are found up the Caren Range.

dane concerns have followed you up. If you take the road to the left and drive as far as possible, at about 18 km (11 mi) there is a trail up 1,318 m (4,350 ft) Mt. Hallowell. At the top, you can enjoy a 360° view from one of BC's last intact forest fire observation towers. Class 3–4.

Pender Harbour: Mt. Hallowell Mine

This trip offers another route to the Caren, if you can surmount an earthen barrier, brave a narrow washout and squeeze past a landslide. We managed it in a Geo Tracker. Take the Malaspina Substation Road, 6 km (3.6 mi) north of PetroCanada gas station (Garden Bay Road turnoff) on the Sunshine Coast Highway at Kleindale. At 1.1 km (.7 mi) take the right fork around the substation. At 8.7 km (5.2 mi) shift into 4WD and take the left fork. Stop at the washout at 11.4 km (6.8 mi) to decide if your vehicle can clear the dirt barrier and negotiate the narrow patch of road above the washout. If you get past the washout, watch for overhanging branches and windfalls which other travellers have cut away, but which might scrape the roof of a big vehicle. The rockslide is at 12.7 km (7.6 mi), where a big boulder leaves not much more than a couple of metres (7 ft) to squeeze past. Keep to the left at the forks at 13.9 km (8.3 mi) and 14.5 km (8.7 mi) and you'll reach the old copper mine and a grand view at 14.8 km (8.9 mi). From this route there are forks and and byways that will take you through the Caren Range, and even onto the Caren Mainline into Halfmoon Bay. Much of this route is steep, and conditions are unpredictable, but it offers a fairly quick and challenging ascent. Class 5–7.

AREA FIVE: POWELL RIVER

Saltery Bay, Hotham Lookout, Brooks Lake

There are far more 4x4 roads around the upper Sunshine Coast than on the lower Sunshine Coast, and the terrain up here is especially pleasing. The roads start the moment you disembark from the Earls Cove/Saltery Bay ferry across Jervis Inlet. As you drive off take the first right on the Saltery Bay Forest Service Road. The route climbs quickly, but when you crest the hill at about 7 km (4.2 mi), the views over Hotham Sound and Jervis Inlet are more than rewarding. If you drive past the lookout and follow the road down into the forest, you'll come across lakes known for good angling, including Brooks Lake. Class 3–5.

Stillwater Bay, Lang Bay

About 10 km (6 mi) from the ferry slip another mainline road heads off to the right. It is the domain of big, *big* trucks. If you've never seen an off-highway logging truck count yourself lucky. They're 14 feet wide and 20 high;

Bear Tooth Mountain, accessible from the top end of Powell Lake.

they can't stop easily and if you meet one, *ditch it fast*! To put it simply, don't use these roads unless you're radio equipped or it's a weekend.

Having said that (again), these roads lead to some amazing back country wonders. If you keep right at the first intersection you'll come to a nice little boat launch on Lois Lake. But by staying on the main road you'll have access to literally hundreds of miles of driveable terrain. If you go past Lois Lake and keep right at around 7 km

*Gorgeous view overlooking Desolation Sound
from the Theodosia area.*

(4.2 mi), you'll be on your way to Khartoum Lake and Freda Lake.

To get to Freda, go left at the first major fork and drive as far as you can go. Freda Lake is 40 km (24 mi) from the pavement, surrounded by stunning alpine scenery and full of fish. Camping here is limited but exceptional. This may be the nicest 4x4-accessible lake on the entire Sunshine Coast. Mt. Freda itself is one of the highest climbable peaks in the area at over 1,800 m (6,000 ft) and a good trail heads up it from the road, courtesy of a Powell River mountaineering club. Class 3–5.

If you skip the Freda–Khartoum cutoff you'll be headed for a half dozen more incredible lakes, a couple of cool canyons and more alpine adventure. Tin Hat Mountain awaits as well as the Eldred River and Horseshoe, Dodd, Windsor and Goat lakes. About 7 km (4.2 mi) from the pavement you'll leave the Mac Blo road by veering left to join the mainline. Offshoot 4x4 roads are too numerous to list, but every weekend of the summer is nowhere near enough time to explore this back country extravaganza. Be warned again, this is good map country. Getting lost up here is no fun. There ain't no gas stations anywhere. There are fairly well marked road signs throughout the area, but you should carry at least three different maps: the Forest Service map for the area, MacMillan Bloedel's and the 1:125,000 topographic. Class 3–7.

Scuttle Bay, Okeover Arm, Theodosia Inlet

About 10 km (6 mi) north of Powell River on Highway 101 is Wilde Road, and 1.5 km (.9 mi) past it is Southview Road. Both head up, over or along the Bunster Range. Wilde Road offers good views behind Powell River as well as access to good canoeing and fishing at Sliammon Lake. Southview Road is just that, a good road for southwest views over the Malaspina Peninsula, Copeland and Savary Islands, Theodosia Inlet and Okeover Arm. Class 3–4.

APPENDIX

For an easy entree to the lower Sunshine Coast on the web try bigpacific.com where you will find links to virtually everything. For the upper Sunshine Coast, try www.discoverpowellriver.com.

TOURIST INFORMATION

Gibsons	886-2325	www.gibsonschamber.com
Sechelt	885-0662	www.secheltchamber.bc.ca
Madeira Park	883-2561	www.penderharbour.org
Powell River	485-4701	www.discoverpowellriver.com
Tourism British Columbia	1-800-663-6000	

PARKS

PROVINCIAL PARKS

ROBERTS CREEK PROVINCIAL PARK: On Highway 101, 14 km (8.4 mi) west of Gibsons. 25 campsites, 24 picnic tables in the day-use area 2 km (1.2 mi) southeast of campground, swimming beach (no lifeguard), sani-station nearby, fishing.

SECHELT INLET MARINE PARKS: 8 marine park sites. All are accessible by boat, some by hiking. Limited development.

Halfway Marine Park	Piper Point Marine Park
Tuwanek Marine Park	Thornhill Marine Park
Nine Mile Point Marine Park	Tzoonie Narrows Marine Park
Kunechin Point Marine Park	Skaiakos Point Marine Park

PORPOISE BAY PROVINCIAL PARK: 4 km (2.4 mi) east and south of Sechelt. 86 campsites, toilets, showers, sani-station, picnic tables. Good swimming (at your own risk), hiking, fishing, scuba diving.

SARGEANT BAY PROVINCIAL PARK: On Redrooffs Road about 10 km (6 mi) from Sechelt. A brand-new park still in development to restore a unique marsh environment almost wiped out by various projects. No camping, limited facilities. Good beach access.

SMUGGLER COVE MARINE PARK: About halfway between Halfmoon Bay and Secret Cove. Access by boat or hike in from the highway. 5 primitive campsites.

GARDEN BAY MARINE PARK: An undeveloped area on the north shore of Pender Harbour at Garden Bay.

FRANCIS POINT PROVINCIAL PARK: 200 acres of undeveloped waterfront on Francis Peninsula in Pender Harbour. This property had just been declared a park at press time so further details were not available.

SKOOKUMCHUCK NARROWS PROVINCIAL PARK: On the northeast tip of the Sechelt Peninsula. Access from Egmont Road. Day use only.

SALTERY BAY CAMPSITE and PICNIC SITE (2 km/1.2 mi away): A short drive from the Saltery Bay ferry terminal off Highway 101. 42 shaded sites, seaside picnic tables, rich shoreline for scuba and skin diving, a boat launching ramp, fishing.

INLAND LAKE: 5 wheelchair accessible cabins and fishing docks for the disabled plus 13 campsites in main site, 2 on trail.

CONFEDERATION LAKE: 1 Rough Cabin Site.

OKEOVER ARM PROVINCIAL PARK: 19 km (11.4 mi) north of Powell River on the east side of Malaspina Peninsula, overlooking Okeover Arm. There are only 3 campsites on the 5-ha (12.5-acre) site.

MUNICIPAL CAMPSITES

WILLINGDON BEACH CAMPSITE: A popular Powell River campground close to the Westview shopping area and the Recreational Complex. It has a sandy beach, playground and covered cooking area. 485-2242

FOREST SERVICE PARKS/CAMPSITES

Forest service campsites are informal, with a minimum of facilities. They charge an $8-$10 camping fee and offer annual passes for $22-27. For more information phone: 1-800-663-7867.

Lower Sunshine Coast

MOUNT RICHARDSON: A medium-sized site on Richardson Lake north of Sechelt. Access on weekends only or after 8 p.m. Four-wheel-drive access only.
LYON LAKE: A semi-forested site. Access is via the Halfmoon Bay Forest Road.
KLEIN LAKE: A medium-sized site on the north end of the Sechelt Peninsula.

Upper Sunshine Coast

KHARTOUM LAKE: A quiet lakeshore site with a gravel boat launch. Basic facilities. Access on weekends only, or after 8 p.m.
NANTON LAKE: A large forested site on the south shore of Nanton. Access on weekends only, or after 8 p.m.
DODD LAKE: Sunny sites and a gravel boat launch. Access on weekends only, or after 8 p.m.
BOBS LAKE: A small forested site at the south end of Bobs Lake on Texada Island.
DINNER ROCK: A small scenic park overlooking a coral-coloured rock beach, 25 km (15 mi) northwest of Powell River.

MUNICIPAL AND REGIONAL PARKS
Lower Sunshine Coast

WHISPERING FIRS: Gibsons area. Sunshine Coast Highway to Oceanview Drive, just north of Gibsons. Playgrounds, nature trails, picnic sites, washrooms, barbecues, outdoor shelter, potable water.
CLIFF GILKER PARK: Roberts Creek area. Next to the golf course on Sunshine Coast Highway. Playground, picnic sites, washrooms, trails, sports fields, hiking.
CONNOR PARK: Halfmoon Bay area. Redrooffs Road to Westwood and Northwood. Playground, picnic sites, trails, sports fields, washrooms, potable water on 43.5 hectares (109 acres).
COOPER'S GREEN: Halfmoon Bay area. A waterfront park at Redrooffs Road and Fisherman Road. Playground, picnic sites, washrooms, swimming, scuba diving, boat launch.
BAKER'S BEACH PARK: Pender Harbour. Follow Francis Peninsula Road to Warnock Road to the end of Davis Road. Five acre waterfront park, swimming.
JOHN DALY PARK: Pender Harbour area. On Roosen Road off Garden Bay Road. Nature trails, picnic sites. A good place to observe salmon spawning in November and December.

SUNSHINE & SALT AIR

KATHERINE LAKE PARK: Pender Harbour area. On Garden Bay Road. Camping, washrooms, swimming, RV sites, trails, canoeing.

LIONS PARK: Pender Harbour area. On Sunshine Coast Highway just north of Pender Harbour High School. This is a nice little park with trails and picnic sites.

DAN BOSCH PARK: Ruby Lake area. On Sunshine Coast Highway north of Pender Harbour. Picnic sites, washrooms, biking/walking trails, swimming, potable water, canoeing.

Upper Sunshine Coast

HAYWIRE BAY CAMPSITE: Powell River area. On Powell Lake. Can be reached from the road to Inland Lake (see access to Haywire Bay Trails). Barbecue area, 43 campsites, 35 picnic sites, outdoor toilets, coin-operated showers.

MOWAT BAY: Powell River. See access to Mowat Bay Hike. Lakefront, safe swimming, washrooms, picnic area, playground.

WILLINGDON BEACH: Powell River. See access to Willingdon Beach trails. 80 campsites, some with hookups, toilets, showers, sandy ocean beach, safe swimming, RV sani-stn., playground, picnic area, close to tourist attractions & shopping. 485-2242

SHELTER POINT: Texada Island area. See access to Shelter Point Trail. There are 40 campsites, 35 picnic sites, flush toilets and outdoor showers.

OTHER RECREATION ACTIVITIES

GOLFING

Sunshine Coast Golf & Country Club: On Sunshine Coast Highway at north end of Roberts Creek. 18 holes, public welcome, pro shop, dining lounge. 885-9212.

Sechelt Golf & Country Club: Trail Avenue to Reef Road and Shoal Way, follow signs. 2 km (1.2 mi) from downtown Sechelt. 18 holes, public welcome, driving range, pro shop, cafeteria. 885-3342.

Pender Harbour Golf Club: On Sunshine Coast Highway just north of Garden Bay Road. 9 holes, driving range, public welcome, pro shop, dining lounge, electric carts. 883-9541.

Myrtle Point Golf Course, Powell River: 9 or 18 holes, TwiLite rates; Eighteen-Hole Championship design, par 72. Public welcome, pro shop, driving range, lessons with CPGA pro, power cart rentals, lounge, restaurant. 487-4653.

Putters Mini-Golf: 4800 Marine, across from Willingdon Beach, 485-7166.

CYCLING

Lower Sunshine Coast

On the Edge Biking, 7755 Redrooffs Road, Halfmoon Bay, 885-4888, toll-free: 1-877-322-4888.

Sprockids and Coast Riders (cycling club), Doug Detwiller, Gibsons, 886-0772

Trail Bay Sports, 5504 Trail Avenue, Sechelt, sales, service, 885-2512

Upper Sunshine Coast

Taw's Gun and Cycle, 4597 Marine Drive, Powell River, rentals, repairs, 485-2555

CANOE AND KAYAK RENTALS, INSTRUCTION & INFORMATION

Lower Sunshine Coast

Halfmoon Sea Kayaks, 5646 Mintie Road, Halfmoon Bay, 885-2948
Pedals & Paddles, Tillicum Bay Marina, Sechelt, 885-6440
Sunshine Kayaking Ltd, Molly's Lane, Gibsons, 886-9760

Upper Sunshine Coast

Desolation Sound Resort 483-3592
Edgehill Store (canoes) 483-3909
Good Diving & Kayaking 483-3223
Wolfson Creek (both) 487-1699

BOAT CHARTERS AND RENTALS

Lower Sunshine Coast

Lowe's Resort, 883-2456, toll-free: 1-877-883-2456
Rogue Charters, 883-1113
Tzoonie Outdoor Adventures, 885-9802
Gambier Island Water Taxi, 886-8321
Garden Bay Marine Services, 883-2722
Madeira Marina, 883-2266
Malibu Yatch Charters, 883-2003
Sunshine Coast Tours, 883-2280

Upper Sunshine Coast

Sailboats
Ragged Island Charters Ltd 604-483-9173, Pager 414-9266

Power Boats
Cedar Lodge Resort, 483-4414 fax 483-7942
Christy Cove, 487-0890
Desolation Sound Resort, 483-3592 fax 483-7942
Destiny Charters, 485-9616
Gail Warning Charters, 487-4446
Kaptain Wave Charters, 485-4380
Papa Bear's Vacations, 483-8224 fax 853-3135
Powell Lake Taxi & Charters, 414-0800
Pristine Charters, 483-4541
Y-Knot Campsite & Charters, 483-3243

SCUBA DIVING AND SNORKELLING

For further reading on scuba diving on the Sunshine Coast, see the relevant section of Betty Pratt-Johnson's *141 Dives*. Check the Yellow Pages of your telephone directory for listings.

SWIMMING POOLS
Gibsons and District Swimming Pool, 886-9415
Pender Harbour Aquatic & Fitness Centre, 883-2612
Powell River Recreation Complex (swimming pool, skating rink & fitness centre), 485-2891

SPORTS/NATURE ORGANIZATIONS
Lower Sunshine Coast
Astronomy Club, Neil Sandy, 886-8356
Elphinstone Aero Club, George Croteau, 885-7031
Elphinstone Flying Club, Alex Swanson, 885-4458
Forest Walkers, Pat Ridgeway, 886-8820
Forest Watch, Adrian Belshaw, 886-2253
Suncoast Racquet Club, Diane Anderson, 888-2385
Sunshine Coast Equestrian Club, Sonya McKenzie, president, 885-7810
Sunshine Coast Power & Sail Squadron, Ford Clark, instructor, 886-7201
Sunshine Coast Rod & Gun Club, Gary Berdahl, 886-7231
Whiskeyjack Nature Tours, Tony Greenfield (bird specialist), 885-7869

Upper Sunshine Coast
Flying Club, 485-6916
Hiking Club, Tony Mathews, 483-3906
Rod and Gun Club, 485-4459

MUSEUMS
Lower Sunshine Coast
Elphinstone Pioneer Museum, 886-8232
Gibsons Landing Heritage Society, Nest Lewis, 886-7573
Sunshine Coast Maritime Museum and Maritime History Society, 886-4114
Tems Swiya Museum (Sechelt Indian Band) 885-8991

Upper Sunshine Coast
Powell River Historical Museum, Teedie Gillette, 485-2222
Powell River Forestry Museum & Beach Walk, Rudi Van Zwaaij 483-9828

THE ARTS
Lower Sunshine Coast
Festival of the Written Arts (Sechelt), 885-9631
Raven's Cry Theatre (Sechelt), 885-4597
Rockwood Centre (Sechelt), 885-2522
Sunshine Coast Arts Centre (Sechelt), 885-5412

Upper Sunshine Coast
Powell River Academy of Music, 483-3346
Powell River Fine Arts Association, Evergreen Theatre (Powell River), 485-2891

TRANSPORTATION

FERRIES

BC Ferries run daily between Horseshoe Bay and Langdale, Langdale and
Gambier Island, and between Earls Cove and Saltery Bay.

Langdale terminal, 886-2242
Saltery Bay terminal, 487-9333
Horseshoe Bay terminal, 921-7414

The Comox ferry runs four times daily from Little River on Vancouver Island to
the Westview wharf in Powell River.

Westview terminal, 485-2943

BUS SERVICE

Malaspina Coach Lines runs buses twice daily from the Vancouver bus depot
through to Powell River, return; with an additional round trip from Vancouver
to Sechelt. The buses make request stops all along the route.

Vancouver 682-6511
Gibsons depot, 886-7742
Sechelt depot, 885-2217
Powell River depot (Westview), 485-5030

Sunshine Coast Transit system provides daily bus transportation between
Sechelt, Gibsons and Langdale and less frequent service to Halfmoon Bay and
Secret Cove. 885-3234
Powell River Regional Transit System offers daily bus service within the munici-
pality, 485-4287
HandyDart, para transit, provides service north to Wildwood, south to Roberts
Road. Saltery Bay on Monday only; Texada on Thursday only. Phone 483-2008
one day ahead.
In the Powell River area, courtesy buses offer scheduled pick-ups from Beach
Gardens, Westview Boat Harbour and Willingdon Beach Campsite.

TAXI SERVICE

Gibsons

Sunshine Coast Taxi, 886-7337

Sechelt

Blue Wave, 885-3525
Sunshine Cabs, 885-3666

Powell River

Powell River Taxi Co., 483-3666

AIR SERVICE

Lower Sunshine Coast

Pacific Wings Airlines flies between Sechelt, Vancouver, Victoria, Nanaimo,
Jervis Inlet and Campbell River. 885-2111 or 1-866-885-2111.

Upper Sunshine Coast

Pacific Coastal Airlines flies daily from Vancouver to the Westview Airport,
483-2107 Toll Free: 1-800-663-2872

AIRCRAFT CHARTERS
Sechelt Peninsula
Airspan Helicopters Ltd., 885-7474
Coast Western, 885-4711

Powell River
Bates Air Ltd, 485-2551, toll-free: 1-877-577-8778
Ocean View Helicopters, 485-7135
Pacific Coastal Airlines, 483-2107, toll-free: 1-800-663-2872
Panther Helicopters, 485-6634

PUBLIC SERVICES

Municipalities and Regional Districts
Gibsons, 886-2274
Sechelt, 885-1986
Sechelt Indian Government District, 885-2273
Regional District of the Sunshine Coast, 885-2261
Powell River Municipal Office, 485-6291
Powell River Regional District, 483-3231
Sliammon (Indian) Band Office, 483-9646

Provincial and Federal Government Agencies
Coast Guard Auxiliary:
Unit 14, Gibsons, 886-7168 or 886-8828
Powell River (Marine & Aircraft Distress), 1-800-567-5111 (*311 on a cellular phone)

Conservation Officer:
Sechelt, 740-5033
Powell River, 485-3612

Environment, Lands and Parks, Ministry of:
Environment, 1-800-663-7867
Lands, 1-800-665-2399
Parks (Porpoise Bay), 885-9019

Fisheries & Oceans, Department of (DFO):
Lower Sunshine Coast, 883-2313
Upper Sunshine Coast, 485-7963

Forest Service (Maps, Forest Service Recreation Sites, Logging Road info):
Sechelt, 740-5005
Powell River, 485-0700
To report a forest fire, 1-800-663-5555

Government Agent (Good source for topographical maps):
Sechelt, 885-5187
Powell River, 485-3622
Other communities call Enquiry BC (1-800-663-7867) and request transfer to nearest Government Agent.

Health Units:
Gibsons, 886-5600
Sechelt, 885-5164
Powell Community Health Council, 485-3207
Environmental Health Protection, 485-8850

Hospitals:
Sechelt, St. Mary's Hospital, 5544 Sunshine Coast Highway, 885-2224
Powell River General Hospital, 485-3211

Highway Condition Information (24 hrs), 1-900-565-4997
Wildlife Violations Reporting (24 hrs), 1-800-663-9453

Motor Vehicle Branch:
Gibsons, 886-3379
Sechelt, 885-2291
Powell River, 485-7931

OTHER COMMUNITY SERVICES

(Lower) Sunshine Coast Community Services, 885-5881
SPCA (Gibsons), Clint Davy, 886-2273
SPCA (Powell River), 485-0891

CALENDAR OF EVENTS

These are some of the events that are established enough to be considered annual. Since the specific dates are often not pinned down until a few months before the event, we have included telephone numbers to contact for information. Where no number is given call 485-4701 for Powell River (PR) events.

January
New Year's Day Polar Bear Swim, Davis Bay, Sechelt.
Minor Hockey Jamboree, Recreation Complex, Powell River.
February
Oldtimers Hockey Tournament, Recreation Complex, Powell River.
Dakota Bowl Winter Carnival, Sechelt.
March
Powell River Music Festival, Evergreen Theatre, Powell River.
March/April
April Fools Run, half marathon, Sechelt to Gibsons.
Jazz Festival, Evergreen Theatre, Powell River, 483-3346.
Powell River Chorus Spring Concert, 485-6956
April
Jazz Summit, sponsored by the Powell River Academy of Music, Evergreen Theatre, Powell River, 483-3346.
Open Air Market Seasonal Opening, Powell River, Sat. 10:30, Sun. 12:30.
Sunshine Coast Music Festival, Sechelt, 885-9010.

May
Victoria Day, May Day Celebrations in Pender Harbour.
Home Show, Recreation Complex Arena, Powell River, 485-4701.
Far Off Broadway Spring Production, Powell River.
Maritime History Weekend, Gibsons.
United Way Golf Tourney, Powell River,483-3465
Choirs in Concert, Academy of Music, Evergreen Theatre, Powell River. 485-9633
June
Men's Malaspina Amateur Golf Tournament, Myrtle Point Golf Course, Powell River, 487-4653.
Dance Review, Evergreen Theatre, Powell River, 485-9633
July
July 1 Canada Day celebrations. Gibsons, Sechelt and Powell River.
Kathaumixw International Choral Festival, even years only, Recreation Complex, Powell River.
Halfmoon Bay Country Fair, Halfmoon Bay, 885-5740.
Gibsons Sea Cavalcade.
Gibsons Yacht Club Regatta.
Gambier Island Craft Fair, 886-9653.
Logger Sports, World Championships, Willingdon Beach, Powell River, 487-4175.
July/August (weekend of lowest tide)
Sandcastle Weekend, Ballfield, Gillies Bay, Texada Island.
Summer Curling Bonspiel, Recreation Complex, Powell River, 483-9551.
August
Blackberry Festival: Street party & Vintner's contest, Powell River, 485-4701.
Powell River Sea Fair, 485-4701.
Festival of the Written Arts, Canadian authors and literary events, Rockwood Centre, Sechelt, 885-9631.
Sunshine Coast Arts Council Craft Fair, held during the Festival of the Written Arts, Hackett Park, Sechelt.
Coast Mission boats reunion, sponsored by Sundowner Inn, Pender Harbour, (odd-numbered years only) 883-9676.
Powell River Sea Fair, 485-4701
September
Labour Day Weekend, Sunshine Folkfest, Palm Beach, Powell River.
Ladies' Malaspina Amateur Golf Tournament, Myrtle Point Golf Course.
Pender Harbour Jazz Festival, 883-2403.
Sechelt Celebration Days.
Sunshine Coast Fall Fair, Gibsons.
Powell River Fall Fair, Exhibition Park, 485-4923
November
Townsite Heritage Days. Powell River, 483-3901.
Roberts Creek Christmas Fair.
December
Light the Lights Festival, Rockwood Centre, Sechelt, 885-9631.
Sunshine Coast Arts Council Christmas Craft Fair, Sechelt, 885-5412.
Carol Ships. Gibsons, Sechelt and Pender Harbour.
Christmas Craft Fair and Carol Ships, Powell River, 485-4701.
Carols by Candlelight, Dwight Hall, Powell River, 485-2891

FURTHER READING ABOUT THE SUNSHINE COAST

BRADLEY, R. KEN and SOUTHERN, KAREN, *The Powell River Railway Era*, BC Railway Historical Association, Victoria, 2000.

CALHOUN, BRUCE, *Mac and the Princess: The Story of Princess Louisa Inlet*, Ricwalt Publishing, Seattle, 1976.

CLARK, LEWIS J., *Wild Flowers of British Columbia*, Gray's Publishing Ltd., Sidney, BC, 1973.

CLEMENTS, PAUL, and BURTON, CLYDE, Powell River Birdlist, The, Powell River Naturalists, Powell River, 2000

CUMMINGS, AL & BAILEY-CUMMINGS, JO, *Gunkholing in the Desolation Sound and Princess Louisa Inlet*, Edmonds, WA, Nor'westing Inc., 1989.

DAWE, HELEN, *Helen Dawe's Sechelt*, Harbour Publishing, Madeira Park, 1990.

DROPE, DOROTHY and BODHI, *Paddling the Sunshine Coast*, Harbour Publishing, Madeira Park, 1997.

FARRAND, JOHN, ed., *The Audubon Society Master Guide to Birding*, Volumes 1-3, Random House, Toronto, 1985.

FRITH, ELLEN and TROWER, PETER, *Rough and Ready Times: The History of Port Mellon*, Howe Sound Pulp and Paper Ltd., Port Mellon, BC, 1993.

GRAHAM, DONALD, *Lights of the Inside Passage: A History of BC's Lighthouses and their Keepers*, Harbour Publishing, Madeira Park, 1986.

HAMMOND, DICK, *Tales From Hidden Basin*, Harbour Publishing, Madeira Park, 1996.

HARBORD, HEATHER, ed. and ABBOTT, ELIZABETH, illustrator, Nature Sites, Powell River Naturalists, The, Powell River, 2000

HENRY, TOM, *The Good Company: An Affectionate History of the Union Steamships*, Harbour Publishing, Madeira Park, 1994.

HOSIE, R.C., *Native Trees of Canada*, Fitzhenry & Whiteside, Don Mills, Ont., 1979.

KELLER, BETTY C., and LESLIE, ROSELLA, *Bright Seas, Pioneer Spirits: The Sunshine Coast*, Horsdal & Schubart, Victoria, 1996.

KENNEDY, DOROTHY and BOUCHARD, RANDY, *Sliammon Life, Sliammon Lands*, Talonbooks, Vancouver, 1983.

LAMBERT, BARBARA A, Chalkdust & Outhouses: West Coast Schools, 1893-1950, Barbara Ann Lambert Productions, 2000

LAMBERT, BARBARA A, In Paradise: West Coast Short Stories, Barbara Ann Lambert Productions, 1998

LYONS, C.P., *Trees, Shrubs and Flowers to Know in British Columbia*, Fitzhenry & Whiteside, Richmond Hill, Ont., 1991.

PETERSON, LESTER, *The Gibsons Landing Story*, Peter Martin Books, Toronto, 1962.

PETERSON, LESTER, *The Story of the Sechelt Nation*, Sechelt Indian Band, Sechelt, 1990.

ROBERTS CREEK HISTORICAL SOCIETY, *Remembering Roberts Creek, 1889–1955*, Harbour Publishing, Madeira Park, 1978.

ROBERTS, HARRY, *The Trail of Chack Chack*, Carlton, New York, 1968.

ROGERS, FRED, *Shipwrecks of British Columbia*, Douglas & McIntyre, Vancouver, 1973.

RUSHTON, GERALD, *Echoes of the Whistle: An Illustrated History of the Union Steamship Company*, Douglas & MacIntyre, Vancouver, 1980.

SOUTHERN, KAREN, and BIRD, PEGGY, *Pulp, Paper and People: 75 Years of Powell River*, Powell River Heritage Research Association, Powell River, BC, 1990.

SOUTHERN, KAREN, *The Nelson Island Story*, Hancock House, Surrey, BC, 1987.

TAYLOR, HARRY, Ed., *Powell River's First 50 Years*, Powell River News, Powell River, BC, 1960.

THOMPSON, BILL, *Boats, Bucksaws and Blisters: Pioneer Tales of the Powell River Area*, Powell River Heritage Research Association, Powell River, BC, 1993.

THOMPSON, BILL, *Once Upon a Stump: Times and Tales of Powell River Pioneers*, Powell River Heritage Research Association, Powell River, BC, 1990.
WHITE, HOWARD, ed., *Raincoast Chronicles, First Five*, Harbour Publishing, Madeira Park, 1976.
WHITE, HOWARD, ed., *Raincoast Chronicles Six/Ten*, Harbour Publishing, Madeira Park, 1994.
WHITE, HOWARD, ed., *Raincoast Chronicles Eleven Up*, Harbour Publishing, Madeira Park, 1994.
WHITE, HOWARD, ed., *Raincoast Chronicles 17*, Harbour Publishing, Madeira Park, 1996.
WHITE, HOWARD and SPILSBURY, JIM, *Spilsbury's Coast: Pioneer Years in the Wet West*, Harbour Publishing, Madeira Park, 1987.
WHITE, HOWARD, *The Sunshine Coast*, Harbour Publishing, Madeira Park, 1996.
WOLFERSTAN, W., *Cruising Guide to BC, Volume 3: Sunshine Coast*, Whitecap Books, Vancouver, 1982.

ACKNOWLEDGEMENTS

The authors and editors would like to thank Vince Bracewell, Pam Barnsley, Rita Percheson and Sandy Barrett, authors of the original 1977 *Hiking the Sunshine Coast*. Thanks to Bob Rebantad and Gerard Nachtegaele of the Forest Service for providing information, text and maps for many of the hiking and biking trails. Fred W. Inglis provided text and information on the Elphinstone Trails. Tony Greenfield of Whiskeyjack Nature Tours provided his expert advice on the hikes. Monika Acciaroli of Tidalwave Diving, Wayne McMahon, and Bryce Christie of Sunshine Coast Tours provided text and information regarding diving. Most of the canoe/kayak trips in this book are extracted from *Paddling the Sunshine Coast*, by Dorothy and Bodhi Drope, Harbour Publishing, 1997.

For the upper Sunshine Coast, special thanks also goes to Carol Hamilton and assistants at the Powell River Visitors' Bureau for all the helpful information and details they supplied, and Teedie Gillette of the Powell River Museum and Archives, for the use of the historic photos.

Keith Thirkell and David Lee, authors of the four-wheeling section, wish to thank Barbara Watt, Shad Light and Skookum Chrysler for their services, time and use of vehicles.

The contributions of the many photographers is also greatly appreciated (see page 4 for photo credits).

EMERGENCY PHONE NUMBERS

Lower Sunshine Coast (Port Mellon to Egmont)
Fire 911
Police 911
Ambulance 911

Upper Sunshine Coast (Saltery Bay to Lund)
Fire 485-4321
Police 485-6255
Ambulance 485-4211

Texada Island (Van Anda & Gillies Bay)
Fire 485-4321
Police 486-7717
Ambulance 485-4211

To report a forest fire 1-800-663-5555
Poison Control Centre 1-800-567-8911
Search and Rescue . . . . .1-800-567-5111, Cellular *311.
Provincial Emergency program . . . . .1-800-663-3456, Cellular*3722.

If you find an injured animal on the lower Sunshine Coast, call the Sunshine
Coast Rehabilitation Society . . . . .604-740-3305.

INDEX